EMOTIONAL INTELLIGENCE

A Practical Guide to Making Friends With Your Emotions and Raising Your Eq

(Most Effective Tips and Tricks on Self Awareness, Controlling Your Emotions)

Charles Bennett

Published by Chris David

Charles Bennett

All Rights Reserved

Emotional Intelligence: A Practical Guide to Making Friends With Your Emotions and Raising Your Eq (Most Effective Tips and Tricks on Self Awareness, Controlling Your Emotions)

ISBN 978-1-77485-362-7

All rights reserved. No part of this guide may be reproduced in any form without permission in writing from the publisher except in the case of brief quotations embodied in critical articles or reviews.

Legal & Disclaimer

The information contained in this book is not designed to replace or take the place of any form of medicine or professional medical advice. The information in this book has been provided for educational and entertainment purposes only.

The information contained in this book has been compiled from sources deemed reliable, and it is accurate to the best of the Author's knowledge; however, the Author cannot guarantee its accuracy and validity and cannot be held liable for any errors or omissions. Changes are periodically made to this book. You must consult your doctor or get professional medical advice before using any of the suggested remedies, techniques, or information in this book.

Upon using the information contained in this book, you agree to hold harmless the Author from and against any damages, costs, and expenses, including any legal fees potentially resulting from the application of any of the information provided by this guide. This disclaimer applies to any damages or injury caused by the use and application, whether directly or indirectly, of any advice or information presented, whether for breach of contract, tort, negligence, personal injury, criminal intent, or under any other cause of action.

You agree to accept all risks of using the information presented inside this book. You need to consult a professional medical practitioner in order to ensure you are both able and healthy enough to participate in this program.

Table of Contents

INTRODUCTION 1

CHAPTER 1: WHAT IS EMOTIONAL INTELLIGENCE? 3

CHAPTER 2: THE EMOTIONAL INTELLIGENCE PROCESS 16

CHAPTER 3: THE BALLAD OF THE MAN WHO WON'T PAY ATTENTION 33

CHAPTER 4: EMOTIONAL INTELLIGENCE METHODS & TECHNIQUES 37

CHAPTER 5: DISTINGUISHING BETWEEN FREEDOM AND DISCIPLINE 44

CHAPTER 6: BUILDING EMOTIONAL INTELLIGENCE 67

CHAPTER 7: THE REASONS YOU HAVE TO TAKE RESPONSIBILITY AND CREATE PERSONAL LIMITS 89

CHAPTER 8: IDENTIFYING YOUR STRENGTHS AND WEAKNESSES 97

CHAPTER 9: BECOMING ACQUAINTED OF YOUR OWN EMOTIONS 103

CHAPTER 10: EMOTIONAL INTELLIGENCE 109

CHAPTER 11: INSPIRE MOTIVATION 123

CHAPTER 12: THE EQ FITNESS PROGRAM: WORKOUTS FOR THE DEVELOPMENT OF EMOTIONAL INTELLIGENCE 130

CHAPTER 13: TAKING EMOTIONAL INTELLIGENCE TO WORK 139

CHAPTER 14: SELF-MANAGEMENT 160

CHAPTER 15: THE SOCIAL MANAGEMENT AND RESPONSIBILITIES 179

Introduction

The premise of the book's title is that many of us believe that our thoughts are out in our hands. Our minds are overwhelmed by negativity, negative thinking attitude and self-esteem issues, and we've allowed ourselves to think that we are in no position to alter this.

We are able to change the way that we think and are the best equipped to make that change. With a few simple steps we can alter our perspective from one of cynical negativity to one of optimism. The benefits that can be gained from a positive attitude can range from improved health and reduced stress levels to increased inter-relational skills that improve our work as well as social situations.

This book is designed to guide us into taking a look at the world in front of us with a fresh set of eyes. Eyes which are open to the amazing things we have , and the vast opportunities which is available to us. It gives us a few simple strategies that can help us alter the way we look at your life. It also addresses the challenges we face and the negative mindset we often carry with our. Unbound from the limiting mental burden of negative thoughts and limiting beliefs, we suddenly are in a position to recognize new possibilities and react to these opportunities with a renewed sense of positivity. We are soon in a world of prosperity that was always there but we've become inaccessible to.

Chapter 1: What is Emotional Intelligence?

Emotional Intelligence, also known as EQ, is the capacity to detect, comprehend how to use and manage emotion in a constructive and positive manner to improve communication, deal with difficulties, ease anxiety, befriend others , and manage conflict. The spectrum of emotional intelligence can be vast and encompasses a range of aspects of our life, such as the way we conduct ourselves and interact with other people.

If you're emotionally smart and have a good understanding of your emotions, you will be at recognizing your personal emotional state and your emotional condition of other people. Knowing the emotional state of others who are around you will allow you better connect with them, gain more success, build better relationships, and lead happier life in general.

In comparison to what we refer to as the intelligence quotient, or IQ emotional intelligence is thought to be more crucial to achieving satisfaction and happiness in your professional and personal life. The ability to recognize and interpret signals from others and to respond correctly will ultimately determine how far you reach in your professional and personal goals to achieve success. This is why it's crucial to build an emotional intelligence which will enable you to comprehend how to negotiate, empathize, and connect with other people.

The categories of emotional intelligence

Researchers studying emotional intelligence have discovered that five main kinds of skills related to emotional intelligence.

Self-Awareness

Self-awareness is the ability to understand your feelings and the effect they have on not just your thinking but also your actions as well. By being aware of yourself, you'll be able to identify the strengths as well as weaknesses. It is an essential component in your psychological intelligence. Being aware of yourself can assist you in building confidence in yourself.

Self-Regulation

Self-regulation is the ability to control your impulsive behavior and emotions under control. It is an additional aspect that makes up emotional intelligence. Self-management isn't a way to stop feelings from occurring however, it lets you decide how long an emotion lasts. Understanding how to manage your emotions in a healthy way and adapting to the changing environment and keeping to commitments are only a few important elements of self-regulation.

There are a variety of techniques you can employ to manage negative emotions such as anger, anxiety, and depression at low levels. One of these methods is meditation and casting situations in a positive light. Self-regulation includes the following qualities:

* Self-control

* Credibility

* Conscientiousness

* Adaptability

* Innovation

Motivation

Motivation is the inner process that drives you towards the target. This type of emotional intelligence requires you to establish specific goals, establish an established path to reach the goals you have set, as well as maintain a positive mindset. Every person has a predisposition to an optimistic or negative outlook however, with a little determination, you can change the way you think in a positive perspective. Any negative thought that enters your mind can be changed positively to assist you in achieving your objectives. Motivation is comprised of the following:

* Achievement drive

* Affirmation

* Initiative

* Optimism

Empathy

Empathy is the ability to recognize the needs emotions, needs, and concerns of other people, and it is an essential component that is a part of the emotional intelligence. Empathy lets you recognize emotions and power dynamics of groups which will help you react to the actions of others more effectively. Empaths are adept in developing others, serving orientation, leveraging diversity and have a keen understanding of politics.

Social Skills

Social skills are the final class that is a part of the emotional intelligence. Social skills, often referred to as relationship management refers to the ability to improve interpersonal skills that dramatically increase your odds of having a prosperous career and in life. With a global economy and the accessibility to knowledge and information it is vital to be able to communicate effectively for you to to understand and empathize with people and be successful in a team environment. Alongside conflict management having excellent social skills will enable you to:

* Influence other people

* Contact

* Create bonds

* Lead

Psychologists are of the opinion the fact that IQ alone isn't enough for getting happiness and success in life. According to research that show your IQ is just 10-25 percent of your success however, emotional intelligence is about 75 percent. Studies have also revealed that people with high EQ scores perform more effectively at work more confident, and are better leaders. These factors have all resulted in the conclusion that EQ is vital and could dramatically improve a person's performance as well as personal growth.

The benefits of high emotional intelligence

Being a person with a high level of emotional intelligence could make you stand out from others and enable you to make the most of your opportunities. There are many benefits that can be gained to your life because of an emotional intelligence that is high. The good news is that everyone who is willing and able to enhance the EQ levels, provided that you willing to work hard and work on it.

There exist people who are exceptionally intelligent, but they're not satisfied or have a fulfilling life. There are people who are excelling in school but in their relationships with others they're not very good. This is due to the fact that although they may possess a good IQ however, they're emotional intelligence not as high. There are numerous things emotional intelligence can assist you to achieve, such as the following.

Personal Performance

The ability to be emotionally intelligent is considered the key ingredient for your success. It equips you with the ability to handle your own affairs as well as those of others effectively. The ability to be emotionally intelligent gives you techniques and tools that will help you become more aware of your personal feelings and teach you the art of managing your feelings, both positive and negative which improves your personal effectiveness.

Thinking Skills

What makes a problem difficult to resolve may not be the complexity of the issue however, it is the view that you're using. Problems that have been solved in the past can be solved by replacing outdated views with fresh perspectives. The ability to be emotionally intelligent also aids in improving your strategic thinking skills and the ability to motivate and inspire your team.

Professional Relations

With a greater emotional intelligence you'll be able to be able to better understand what drives people. This is vital in creating an harmonious and positive working environment and interpersonal relationships. By increasing you emotional intelligence, the capability to connect with others and to communicate better with other people will increase. This, in turn, will improve your professional relationships.

Capacity for Leadership

Effective leadership requires you to be able to empathize and understand your employees. Emotional intelligence can provide you with strategies that are essential in convincing, inspiring motivation, inspiring, and motivating others. The most important factor that determines the success of any type of leadership is how well you are aware of the feelings of others and how well you react to their emotions. This will significantly increase satisfaction and help create an atmosphere for better workplace relationships.

Physical Health

Your emotional intelligence can have an impact on your overall health. The management of stress is closely connected to your state of mind provides you with the capability to respond positively when faced with challenges in your daily life. This is vital as stress can lead to weakening your physical capabilities and reducing the immune system and eventually reducing your enjoyment of living.

Mental Well-Being

The way you think and the outlook that you take on life is affected by your emotional intelligence. If you're lacking EQ it is likely that you suffer from depression, anxiety, and mood shifts. It will eventually erode your confidence and enthusiasm which can cause your life to become boring and miserable. Your mental stability is typically at its best at times when your entire faculties not just the ability to comprehend the emotions you feel are functioning properly.

Conflict Management

There is no way to avoid conflicts. But, your ability to resolve any disagreement is entirely dependent on your awareness of the emotions of those who are involved. If you are able to understand and empathize with views and feelings of the parties involved who are involved in the dispute It becomes easier to resolve these situations, or stop they from occurring at all. A high level of emotional intelligence helps us become better negotiators as it allows you to gain insight into the needs and requirements of the participants in the dispute. If you are aware of the bones of contention, solving conflicts becomes much more straightforward.

Success

The ability to concentrate on a specific goal is the result of your internal motivations and confidence in yourself. Greater degrees of emotion intelligence provide you with self-control and ensure that you stay on the right track toward achieving your objectives. Additionally, it helps you create an improved support system and persevere with a remarkable level of resilience and overcome the obstacles that can hinder your accomplishment. The person who is emotionally intelligent is able to delay immediate satisfaction and be focused on the long-term effects of a particular course of action, which increases the likelihood of success.

The field of emotional intelligence continuing to attract research by various experts, but what is certain that emotions play a significant contribution to the overall quality of our professional and personal life. The technological advancements have made it easier to comprehend information but it has not substituted our capacity to understand and manage our emotions.

Chapter 2: The Emotional Intelligence Process

Once we have a better understanding of the meaning of emotional intelligence and what it means to your daily life, let's look at the way it functions. In this chapter, we're going to explore the intricate and in-depth processes that determine the emotional intelligence of you. It is crucial to start by understanding how your emotional intelligence is linked to your perception of yourself.

Understanding Yourself

Since emotional intelligence is a reflection of your own emotions and emotions are the core of what you're made of and what you are, it is essential to become aware of your own. If you perceive yourself as positive and healthy manner you'll find it easier to build more positive relationships, handle anxiety, and reach your goals. The way you view and perceive yourself can be called self-perception.

Most people believe they know who they are, but the truth is that most do not take the time to understand the person they truly are. The majority of people experience an emotional episode without thinking about the reasons and consequences of their emotions. Self-perception is crucial as it helps you identify the person you really are. It can also help you identify ways to bridge the gap between your current character and who you wish to become.

One who is not conscious of who they are will never comprehend or recognize the people who are around them. If you are looking to increase the quality of your life, then you should learn to increase your self-awareness.

The first step is to write in a journal how you experience every day. Record your feelings at regular intervals throughout the day, and make sure you write down the reasons of your feelings. When you are done with the day, review the notes you've made. This is an excellent method to identify the ways in which your emotions have formed. This means that you will be in a position to take a more detailed and clearer look at how you live your day, what moods that you encounter, as well as the events or people which trigger your emotions. This is the most effective way to master managing your emotions, and figure out ways to utilize them to your advantage.

Self-perception is a concept that can be examined in three distinct ways:

1. Self-regard

This means making sure you take care of your personal needs first and not coming across as egocentric or insecure. Discover your strengths and then use the advantages to gain. This is essential since a person with an excellent self-esteem will be more likely to be respectful of others. If you're unsure the best way to measure your self-esteem then ask a group of individuals you trust and are familiar with you to provide feedback. When you've got the correct and accurate information, you can begin taking steps according to what you are aware of about yourself.

2.Self-awareness

It is the process of identifying your personal emotions and how they affect others who surround you. Self-awareness can also help you recognize the emotional signals that are not verbal from others. If you're highly aware of yourself, you will find that you can remain in greater relationships than someone who isn't.

The best method to improve your self-awareness and practice is to study the facial expressions and expressions of the people in your vicinity. You can also observe their body language in times of emotional anger. To ensure that this exercise is as efficient as you can ensure that you're not actively involved in the emotional scenario. After the emotional exchange is over take a moment to replay the incident through your head, thinking about the way you would have dealt with the situation if you had been active in the situation. This exercise is a great opportunity to practice for occasions when you'll engage in a heated argument with your partner.

3.Self-actualization

This is the process of trying to fulfill the purpose of your life regardless of whether it's personal or professional in nature. It is important to identify the things that add the most meaning to your life, and pursue these goals. This takes a certain amount of courage , which most people are unable to summon. You must make bold choices and take active steps to realize your potential.

What you must undertake is to take a thorough look at the strengths, talents strengths, weaknesses, and abilities. Discover what they are and use them to reach your goals. Find ways to harness your passions for your personal benefit as well as for your loved ones.

Mindfulness is among the most well-known methods to train your mind to enhance the self-perception of your mind. Mindfulness simply means being aware of what is that are happening in your surroundings at any given moment. For example, if are eating your meal, you may take a mindful approach to eating. In this, you take your time chewing as you take in the flavors of each ingredient of the dish. This will allow you to be more in touch with your mood.

Learn to to step away from an emotional exchange and identify what your real feelings are before reacting. Mindfulness can help you perceive yourself because it teaches your mind to concentrate on what is most important in that moment and pay attention to your own thoughts and things that surround you.

Understanding the roots of Empathy

Empathy is thought as one of the fundamental elements for emotional intelligence. You can't claim to be a person of emotional intelligence yet have no empathy. Empathy is the key to creating the bonds between you and others such as your partner family, children, friends or any other person who you love dearly. It could even assist you in resolving conflict with those who are difficult to work with.

Many people believe that empathy is fixed however, the reality is that everyone can learn to become more compassionate. All you require is a little practice.

What is empathy?

Many people are lost when they are asked to distinguish between sympathy and empathy. They're not the same thing. Sympathy is when you show an individual that you value the difficulties they're facing. If, for instance, Jack's mother dies You meet him and tell him, "Jack, I'm very sorry about the loss of your mother." It's a thoughtful and noble gesture that shows you are concerned about the circumstances that occurred to Jack. But, note that the phrase begins with "I" You have declared it to be about yourself!

Here is the point where the distinction between empathy and sympathy is evident. Empathy puts your emotions of another person in the first place. For instance, "Jack, you must be grieving over the loss of your mother." Do you notice how you began by acknowledging the way Jack feels right now? Empathy is not about personal feelings, but it is about understanding the emotions of someone else.

Why is it important to be aware of the differences between the two feelings? The term "sympathy" is employed when you wish to let someone know what you are feeling about a difficult circumstance they're facing. It is a sign that you are concerned and wish to make them feel at ease. So empathy is clearly an goal in itself.

Empathy is not the same as empathy in that it can be a door opener. Empathy is when you wish to get to know someone better and earn their confidence. It's more than showing concern for their current circumstance and a desire to be able to understand what they're experiencing. Empathy improves relationships and allows you to become more intimate with the person. It is a desire to understand the person better and strengthen your connection with them. As opposed to empathy which is the basis of any interaction.

People in the modern world are adept at expressing empathy when tragedy strikes, and it is evident through the way they use social media. People are quick sending messages of sympathy to the victims of earthquakes, tsunamis, hurricanes or famines, as well as flooding across the world.However the thing that is most lacking is genuine compassion that goes beyond "I" remarks in favor of "You" declarations. What number of people do you know who are naturally compassionate? Learn and improve your empathy abilities and you'll surely be different from the rest of the pack.

Knowing what are the Four Skills of Emotional Intelligence

There are four main capabilities that you should acquire to enable you to deal with any situation in an a way that is emotionally sound.

Self-awareness

It is here that you can learn how to discern your emotions and understand their impact on your thoughts as well as your actions. The more you understand yourself and are aware of your emotions and moods, the more likely you are to be confident in yourself. This puts you in a position to increase the emotional intelligence of your.

Self-management

It is the capability to control your spontaneous emotions, behavior and impulses that can occur at any time. Self-management's primary objective is to to manage your emotions when they arise in a healthy and productive way. It is also important to develop the capacity to adjust to unexpected and new situations and make sure all obligations are fulfilled.

Social awareness

It is essential to recognize what people around you are feeling and also their worries and desires. Social awareness is tied to being comfortable in social situations where you interact with people as well as observing their emotional responses and be aware of the kind of personality traits they possess.

Management of relationships

This is where you can develop the ability to keep healthy and solid relationships. It is essential to master the art of to motivate and influence others to be a successful communication expert, handle or resolve disputes, and be an effective team player.

What impact can emotional intelligence have on Your Life

You are now aware of the abilities that emotional intelligence demands. But, it's vital to be aware of the areas of your life that benefit by being more emotionally intelligent. They include:

Mental health The emotional intelligence of your body is a significant factor in how you see things around you as well as the actions you choose to take. If you have an emotional intelligence that is high, you'll experience an increased sense of mental well-being, manifesting by less stress and greater confidence.

Physical health - You might be aware that each time your emotions get out of control or in control, your physical health decreases. The ability to manage your emotions can help you to be in a place in which you manage the emotions you experience in a balanced way, which improves your physical health.

Relations - This is an essential aspect of our lives, and we have to be able to comprehend the emotions of others. Once you've learned to be aware of your own feelings and emotions, you'll be able to make it easier to express these feelings to others that surround you. The ability to recognize emotions helps you understand the emotions of others and enables the person to behave exactly the way you'd want to be treated.

Prosperity - It's not just about financial achievement. Prosperity is about setting goals, pursuing these goals, and reaching them. The development of a high-level in emotional intelligence can be among the most effective ways to accelerate your way to success. You'll feel more confident and more confident in pursuing your goals. Procrastination and time-wasting will become a thing of the past as you be able to focus and have the strength to keep your promises. If you want to be successful in the near future it is likely that you'll have to sacrifice a lot today and an EQ that is high EQ can help you comprehend the importance of this.

Are You emotionally unintelligent?

One of the primary ways to recognize a person who is not emotionally smart is the lack of self-awareness. Someone who is not emotionally intelligent might be in a crowd of people, but will not have any clue how out of tune they are with the rest of the group. The unfortunate truth of having a low the realm of emotional intelligence, is that it is difficult to know how other people perceive your personality. Even more importantly, you may not understand the reasons why your relationships and life are so challenging.

Unintelligent individuals exhibit behavior that make them their biggest enemy. Due to their lack of empathy, their inability to control their thoughts, and insufficient social skills, anything they do can be self-defeating. They're not always happy they aren't able to resolve their own issues and find it extremely difficult to achieve their personal goals.

It is crucial to remember that these characteristics can lead to issues in the real world. People who have low EQ are more likely to have difficulty keeping any intimate or meaningful relationships, aren't able to hold down jobs for long periods, aren't frequently promoted in their jobs and are unable to deal with the stress. Another thing to consider is that just because you are smart does not mean that you can't be low-EQ. Certain individuals have high IQ but have extremely low EQ.

It isn't easy to recognize people with poor emotional intelligence, as most people are adept at impersonating EI capabilities. Certain individuals are able to conceal their weaknesses using simple methods. Simply because someone says that they're aware of their own actions and the people surrounding them doesn't mean it is real.

Here are some common signs that indicate emotionally inept individuals:

Quickly become angry, without even realizing why or how. are feeling so

Aren't aware of the effect of their actions on other people

I am unable to comprehend the emotions of others

Are typically self-centered

It is difficult to control your emotions particularly when stressed

Inspire others to behave as badly

Are you having difficulty maintaining existing relationships or make new people

Overestimate their capabilities and abilities.

Avoided by the majority of people

Does someone who is emotionally inept a hopeless case? Not at all. Everyone can be taught how to improve their EQ with the proper training. If you've recently discovered that you meet the criteria that was mentioned above, don't be concerned. That's why you're reading this book. The chapters in the book will explain the methods to assess the current level of your EQ and the best way to implement to boost your emotional intelligence overall.

Chapter 3: The Ballad of The Man Who Won't Pay Attention

There's a person who doesn't even listen However, more important we have all known someone who caused a lot of damage to their life because they didn't listen. In the end, there's someone who has their life completely in the mud, and is dragged down into the mess until nothing can be saved from the abyss since when it comes right down to the core, everything all comes to listening.

Seriously the guy or girl, they ruin the perfect relationship, lose their dream job or they lost a loved one because they were not paying attention to be attentive and stop themselves from becoming a victim in the process. This is one of the least avoidable troubles and pains that we face in this world. There are plenty of people who are sinking their lives simply because they fail to take responsibility for what's happening to them. They aren't able to face the reality that they're the ones who have been causing the problems in their lives, and assume that it's just a cosmic problem and they're the ones suffering.

Do not be like this man. Don't be that woman. Be the one who is actively involved within their world. Make sure you know the current state of the day-to-day activities and avoid the misery that unnecessarily entangled in some people's lives. I would like you to take a minute to examine you're living your life as it truly is. Moments.

Life is filled with moments. Moments of quiet, moments of excitement and tension, and even moments of chance as well as countless other occasions. Each moment you live through there are other people around you, or you're alone. Take note of the moments of your day-to-day life and note how much time you're spending in solitude, and the amount of time spent with others or with others what amount of time you're just listening instead of trying to get them to talk to you.

If someone is sinking their lives due to an inability to communicate The reality is that they're not paying attention to those in their lives. They're not listening to spouses, to their family members or coworkers or to the people they encounter every day. When you're in the same room and communication begins do you just listen for them to speak, and then formulate your next word and do you also take time to ponder their wordsand ponder the meaning before responding? How do you handle conversations?

Really, take a second to think about it!

Are you someone who listens? Are you able to listen? Or are you one of those people who don't listen and watches time and time again as miscommunications,'forgetful' moments, or being on the wrong page consumes your relationships and leaves you alone and misunderstanding how things got to this point? This is a valid one to think about. Are you someone who isn't able to listen? If you have the answer, then you're sure that you are able to alter the way you listen.

Keep in mind the old saying The first step in solving any issue is to acknowledge that there's a problem. Did you know that? I believe that the statement has some truth too. You are able to take control over your personal life changing the way you interact with people and the good news. The first step towards being more enlightened and have a better communications in your life is studying this book. This means you're already on the right path and you should continue.

Chapter 4: Emotional Intelligence Methods & Techniques

Six Seconds Model

The Six Seconds Model provides a ideal framework for understanding and using emotions efficiently. Through this model of action it is likely to be a substantial increase in efficiency. This model pushes three ideas that follow that of being more aware of your actions as well as the actions of other people, being more deliberate in all you do which will make you feel more deliberate with a purpose for every action you take. This increases productivity. Perhaps the reason for the increase is because people believe they're living their lives with a purpose or a motive.

Know Yourself

This section is designed to assist you in becoming more aware of yourself, and to understand your emotions and how they relate to your actions. You'll become more connected to yourself. Find out more about yourself and then begin to understand yourself more deeply about what you really are. You are indeed an individual, and you may not be able to understand why you do what they do. However, there are usually a few common connections in your life. Get more focused and observe these links.

Decide to react in a shrewd manner

Instead of responding to events in a kind of "autopilot" way attempt to be more attune to your surroundings. As an example, instead responding out of anger, screaming or screaming at someone for the mistake they committed, instead speak in a way which is purposeful. It is possible to make a statement that has an impact. Every single action you take are intentional and well-formulated within your mind.

Make the most of your Actions

Everyone has ambitions in life even if we are yet to comprehend the purpose behind them. Be sure to realize the goals that you are pursuing with your choices. Once you know yourself more deeply, you'll be able to set your intentions on what you do and begin to live your life with a purpose. You can live a lifestyle with integrity and meaning.

Vital Signs Model

The most important indicators of emotional intelligence can be described as results driven by people, based on action. They form the basis for help team leaders and efficient groups and organizations to progress positively.

Important Signs of Performance:

Based on the vital signs model, each high-performing team, company or leader is able to balance the following concepts:

Strategy: having a plan or clear direction for the direction in which one is headed forward, aided by a plan.

Operations: More efficient operational actions can help to clear the way and direction the person or team would like to follow.

Organization: For every single operation, there's an array of complex focused systems and different systems. This creates an impressive sense of organization to the plan.

People: Every organization is powered by the people who initiate the actions. Based on the Vital Signs Model, there is a need for an intricate balance between the people as well as the business as well as a harmony between the strategy and operational. There are specific instances when the company must concentrate its efforts on the specific segment or area. For instance an organization could concentrate on the operation aspect of the launch of a new product. But , the business might lose focus if the organization puts too much emphasis on this particular sector, and not on the primary direction and plan which they created the company to adhere to.

Important Signs of Workplace climate

According to this model the climate of work is extremely crucial in allowing workers to work in efficient ways. The environment can impact work performance greatly and, contrary to culture, it can change quite quickly. For instance, you'd prefer to invest your time and effort in a workplace that were comfortable working in. You would not prefer to work in an unhealthy workplace.

The work environment must be characterized by a level of confidence. A sense of security and security at work encourages people to experiment and risk taking. Innovation only occurs when an individual steps out of their familiar zone.

Motivation: To motivate individuals to push beyond minimum standards, they have to have a sense that they are committed and enthusiasm. The energy they contribute will boost the performance of an organization or company to move forward.

Change: Employees working in an office must possess the capacity to adapt and adapt or change themselves and their environment. With more mental acuity, they are able to do this. They are able to understand what their coworkers feel and be more compassionate to colleagues. They should be able to adjust to changes within the business.

Teamwork: Individuals should be capable of feeling the collective energy of their team members within the workplace. They should feel like they are an integral member of the team, in order to perform at their best.

Execution: Employees must focus on their job, and as a result, be accountable to their behavior. If they do make mistakes, they need to be aware of the place they committed the error and then learn from the mistake. The hope is that learning from their mistake will to avoid repeating the same mistake in the future.

Chapter 5: Distinguishing Between Freedom and Discipline

Swiss psychiatrist Carl Jung, in one of his studies, defined Individualism as the development of consciousness. It's an expression of identity the moment when an individual discovers their own uniqueness that is distinct from the norms of society. The word that is active here is 'consciousness self-realization and personalization in which one is conscious of their individuality. Jung concept applies to people as members of a the group, not an isolated person.

The role of society is crucial in the lives of people. In the study conducted by Jung self-conscious individuals, they showed an enthralling relationship with their peers. The self-conscious person lets himself be aware of the collective unconscious and react with deliberate expression and attitude.

The society provides institutions such as family or marriage, but not in a limited way to these, in order to facilitate the development of individuality. The most significant threat to those who want to be unique is the threat of conformity. Individualism only shows up when someone makes a choice not because society requires the decision, but because one believes that the decision is the right one. The word that is active in this case can be described as "choice". This is a matter of trust and accountability that is essential in following and leadership. Individualism is the most essential element of freedom.

The Behavior and Culture of Individualism

The way people think and behave is strongly influenced by their culture. The study of cross-cultural differences is the similarities between the collective culture and the one that is more individualistic.

Differentialities in both cultures are also important in these research studies.

In the individualist world, the culture is heavily determined by the individual's worth over a society or group. In this way, an individual asserts their own independence and has the freedom of power. The person who is the boss is the self. The behavior of an individual is less on social norms and more on personal preferences. Western Europe are popular for its unique society.

For instance, the pop-culture of a typical musician from Africa that lives in Detroit is RnB/rap. There are instances when other Genre such as classical music are adopted by people of a similar ethnicity and geographic location. The differences, while they exist but is very rare and is greatly dependent on the social institution, e.g. school groups, community groups and religious organizations.

The table below outlines the differences of Individualistic Culture and Societal Culture:

Individualism Society

1 Person's Right take center stage. Society standards are the main focus

2 The most value is given to the independence of a person. The highest value is given to socialization

3 Person who is self-reliant is dependent on social networks

4 Person is an individual is a conformist to the norms of society.

The potential to draw attention on one's personal identity is a pervasive feature of culture that can have significant influence on the efficacy of a societal functions. For example, someone who believes in individualism is likely to value their personal culture and their well-being over the one imposed by the group. Contrary to the group's cultural norms (collective culture) where people are sacrifices to be pleasing themselves to benefit everyone. This distinction between society and individualism affects our behavior in every sector such as career choices as well as product affiliation, and the ability to respond in response to issues of social concern.

The psychologists who study cross-cultural differences are now conscious of the significant impact that behavior and culture have on one's mental health and in turn, vice versa. However, an issue arises when individual preference/choice/culture may cause harm to the greater number of collectives/societies.

"It isn't what you've got and who you're, or the things you do that can make you happy or sad. It's what your thoughts are about the situation." Dale Carnegie Dale Carnegie

The Social Expectations of the People and Social Standards

A society could be defined as a collection of people or individuals who interact with each other both culturally and socially. The members of this group have a common concept of a belief system that may or not be distinct from their personal ideals.These ideas could be formulated by geography, political, cultural, or religiously. They could be influenced by, but not restricted to race, class and gender. The essence of social structures has to do with "grouping" the individual.

Social norms can influence behavior in various ways. The most prevalent and common is the expectation set by the group or society. We often believe that others will behave in a specific way in certain situations.

We often expect others to behave in a specific way in a specific situation. Every society has a standard and appropriate behavior for people to adhere to. The expectations differ between different social groups to another. Someone belonging to a specific group will be expected to follow these norms, regardless of regardless of whether they agree with it or not. It can be difficult to handle situations in which what people feel regarding something can be different from how the society views it.

"All the world's a stage,

All the men and women who are simply players:

They have their exits , as well as their entrances

One man can today plays several roles."
_____ William Shakespeare

What the poem reveals is the social roles played out by a single person. Imagine the different types of roles you are required to take on every day in your life. For instance the role of a father, mother or child, an employer students, friends and so on. Every role comes with an expected manner of conduct that is known as social norms.

10 Most popular Social Norms

1. One must be extremely popular and have lots of friends

2. One should have a Facebook or Twitter account, and be always active.

3. One should be exceptionally skilled or even an expert at a certain ability.

4. You should be extremely productive at all times.

5. One shouldn't be alone, however, one must be in a relationship that can lead to marriage

6. One should be content every day and stay happy all the time.

7. One must plan ahead to accomplish certain things by a certain point in time e.g. get into university before 25, marry before 30 and establish an exit strategy before the age of 60.

8. One should consider the way they dress and look.

9. On must have a specific kind of perspective that is based on their background in the family and income.

10. You must be graduated from an institution of higher learning or a university

A great deal of pressure is felt when a person reaches compliance with these unspoken or unwritten rules. Many people are grappling with the best way to think about these rules and whether we should accept them or not.

Society is a form of organization that has been around since the time of man. It was, remains, and will continue to be the standard rulebook therefore it is impossible to pretend that it didn't exist. But, it shouldn't be a requirement to adhere to this rules so they don't create harm for others.

In America it is legal to possess a firearm, but it is illegal to shoot someone simply because you're having an unlucky day. But, shooting may be justified by self-defense the person who was injured.

Understanding Human Rights and Freedom

Human rights are fundamental sets of freedoms and choices enjoyed by all human beings at the time of birth until the time of death. They are applicable regardless of the place of origin or religious belief. These are rights that cannot be removed by any higher authority, and are only limited in some instances, e.g. in criminal proceedings.

These rights share the same values:

1. Dignity

2. Fairness

3. Respect

4. Independence

They are clearly defined and protected by the law of the state.

The recognition of these values as fundamental rights of all members of humanity is the core of justice and peace throughout the world.

A) Every person is born equal and has the right to be free of their dignity and rights. They are blessed with a sense of and reason; therefore, they must act with respect and respect for each other, in a spirited unity.

b) Everyone has a rightful claim to the rights that is stated in this document, without regard to race color, gender and language, gender or politics, birthplace and social status, and property. There is no distinction based on the jurisdiction of one's nation or status, whether independent self-governing, non-self-governing, or under another sovereignty.

C) Security, liberty, one's life and everybody's right.

d) Everyone is free of slavery or any other form of servitude. Trade of slaves is illegal in any way.

e) Everyone is exempt from any form of torture, cruel and inhumane actions and treatment

f) All people are entitled to be considered a person under the law.

G) Every person is equal under the law and is entitled to the same protection under the law without discrimination.

h) All are entitled to an equal and an effective remedy from national tribunals when they take action that are in violation of the fundamental rights guaranteed to each person by law.

i) All is safe from being subject to arbitrarily detained arrests, exile or detention.

j) All have the right to an open and fair hearing before an independent and impartial tribunals, when determining whether his obligation is met and any crime that is charged against him.

K) Everyone who is accused of committing a crime are , by law innocent and must considered as innocent prior to being being found guilty in a public trial where the accused is entitled to all defense.

l)None should allow interference with their privacy either at home, in their family, or through correspondence. It shouldn't be a threat on the person's integrity also. Everyone is entitled to be protected under law from all forms of attacks of this kind.

m)Everybody is entitled to freely move around and they can live within state borders. Anyone can leave their home nation and go to any country.

n)If you are being targeted, anyone is entitled to request and be granted a asylum in another country. This is not a right that can be exercised when there is a genuine rise in persecution in instances that are not political in nature.

o)Everybody has the right to be a citizen. Everyone should not be denied their nationality, or change their nationality.

p) With no restrictions on the race, nationality or religion, all males and females have a right to marry and create their own family. They have equality in the marriage, and even after it ends. Marriage can only be granted when both parties agree and no one is forced on them to do so. Family is, naturally, the largest social group. It should be protected by government and society.

q) Everybody is able to have property rights independently and with respect to other people. Nobody is denied his property.

R) the freedom to choose your own conscience and of thought, as well as of belief is an equal right to everyone. This includes the right to alter your beliefs or beliefs. Also, the right to impart the same beliefs in private or in public, and to incorporate these beliefs a part of worship and observation.

S) Everyone is entitled to express their opinions freely and freely their views, whether they are seeking or receiving information through any medium, and without interfering.

t)Everybody has the right for peaceful assemblies and group.

u)Everybody has the right to participate in the governance of their country either directly or through the choice of freely or through an elected representative. Every citizen has the right to take part in government services in their country.

v) Anyone who is member of a social or political group is entitled to safety and security in the society. is granted freedom to use these security.

W) Everyone has the right to work and to choose work or career. The employee must be given favorable contract with favorable terms and conditions and be protected from unemployment. Everyone, regardless of race or gender should be paid the same wages for work. Everybody is entitled to become an associate member or a trade union, to defend their interests.

x) Everyone is entitled to have their own way for the wellbeing of their families and of themselves that includes clothing, food, and housing medical treatment and the other public and social services.

y) Everybody has the right to equal access to education

Z) Everyone is able to freely participate in their local culture and take pleasure in sharing objects.

SELL-WILL AND SELF DISCIPLINE

Self-willed people are those who that is not aware of others' will and desires. The majority of the time the public perceives self-willed people as unreliable or domineering. stubborn.They are a challenge to handle due to their determination to make their own choices. Their selfishness isn't rooted in an urge to put their own well-being the first place. A self-willed individual could be the definition of a martyr. However, their self-centeredness stems due to a strong desire to follow what they believe is the right way.

The willpower of a self-willed man is conscious, focused and active. This can be described in three main categories:

* I will this give an individual the courage to dive into something that isn't boring or losing interest or. This is the reason why an individual on a treadmill instead of simply sitting in a couch.

* I WON'T POWER the ability to not succumb to temptation. This power is activated when we decide to not consume chocolate or ice cream if you want to lose weight.

* I WANT POWER , it provides an effect on the future of one's choice. It's the power of focusing on the delay of gratification. The well-known experiment conducted by Stanford marshmallows has shown that people who wait for their gratification to

be delayed have a better life than those who get immediate satisfaction.

The first thing to think about is choosing a self-willed individual;

1. Independence is a major step as you become self-motivated. Someone will tackle problems with a distinct and unique way. She is a lover of challenges and is constantly inventing new methods to deal with these problems. If they reach an point where they require assistance They will be honest and solicit help. It is a good thing to admit mistakes. Someone who is strong-willed isn't concerned about the opinions of others about him, because he considers his own views and thoughts.

2. To be self-willed, one should be aware of all things. Their minds are brimming with knowledge about everything because they continue to learn about these topics. They study events based on their emotional levels and are able to make decisions based on that information. They constantly put puzzle pieces together in

various types of contexts like the sphere of politics or business and trying to understand the meaning of what's happening. They are extremely imaginative and are the designers of amazing ideas.

3They are curious about their surroundings and they challenge every rule imposed by the society. This doesn't necessarily mean they're lawbreakers but it does mean that they're aware of their rights as humans. They aren't happy the fact that they're assumed to be normal.

4 They are very enthusiastic about their pursuits. They'll go to great lengths to realize their goals and dreams since they aren't scared of challenges. They possess a fix-it mindset that is, in the majority of cases, optimistic.They persevere in their pursuits.

Five of them are loyal reliable, trustworthy and loyal. People who are self-motivated have a good moral character and are genuinely concerned for their loved family members. They are only able to trust a few individuals, and they prefer to stay with the chosen few. They are truthful and honest. Because they are adamant about their moral values there is no reason to conceal their actions from the public eye.

6 They place a high value on their privacy and independence. The self-motivated person doesn't want the interference they face when making their own choices. They require space and time to think, which means getting away from the crowd every once every so often. The person who trusts their instincts and let his voice guide them.

7 The greatest critic of a person who is strong-willed is him. This causes them to constantly improve in themselves as they recognize that they could be more effective. This is due to the fact that they are self-confident. They're not afraid to admit failure, which is why they revisit strategies to turn the failure into success, even if it takes longer (i.e. the idea of moving forward).

8 A self-willed individual says less, but does more. They are the only ones who say what they are going to do. They are clear and clear in their words. They speak only after having gathered their thoughts. This makes their words credible. That means their decisions tend to be better than any.

Self-willed and strong-willed are two within the one. To develop a strong will you must first find your self-confidence and believe in oneself. But, one who is self-willed should exercise self-control to keep a calm mental state.

Self-discipline is the key to success.

One of the most important skills to be a leader is self-control. It is crucial and efficient in everyday life and how you handle situations. While everyone is aware of its effectiveness, only a handful of people are skilled in it.

What is self-control?

It's an inner source of power that drives the individual to adhere to them with a great deal of attention. It's about controlling thoughts, actions and feelings. This is essential for all kinds of leadership since it allows leaders to stay with their decision-making without changing their minds. This makes perseverance appear effortless and indicates a great confidence in self-worth and positivity. The leader is confident that he is going to succeed, so invests in determination. The feelings that distract through nature, like laziness, addiction and procrastination, be ignored in life of self-disciplined people.

The daily challenges we face are not unavoidable, and tackling them correctly is ensuring that they don't harm our health and wellbeing of ourselves and the surrounding environment. Whatever strategy or method you choose to employ to deal with issues it is essential to practice patience, perseverance and determination.

Lack of this ability can lead to failure and loss. E.g. someone must have learned discipline to overcome unhealthy habits like drinking, smoking, or a relationships, or else the person won't be able to achieve his goals.

Other benefits of self-discipline

* It helps one not act on the spur of the moment

It assists in fulfilling commitments made to self as well as others.

* It helps overcome procrastination.

* It provides extra motivation even after the initial surge of excitement to begin the project.

* It gets up early to make the most of the short hours of daylight.

Chapter 6: Building Emotional Intelligence

Emotional Intelligence (also sometimes referred to as emotional quotient, or EQ is an individual's capacity to comprehend and use and manage his emotions in a positive manner. It also depends on an individual's ability to react to the feelings of others. This can help you ease your anxiety, be able to communicate effectively and become more empathetic. It also helps you overcome difficulties, and settle disputes.

It is a psychological process which helps people build solid bonds with other people and be successful at school, work and to reach their professional and personal goals. Emotional Intelligence also goes far in helping you understand your emotions and to be more deliberate and to perform more actions. It assists individuals in making more informed decisions about matters that are important to them.

There are several key traits through which emotional intelligence is usually recognized. These are:

* Self-management This is the characteristic in which you can get control of your emotions and thoughts. It is also associated with your ability to manage the emotions you feel in a healthy way, as well as your capacity to make choices and adjust to changing circumstances.

Self-awareness It is the ability which allows you to become conscious of your emotions and their impact on your thinking and attitude. Anyone with this trait can recognize the strengths and weaknesses of his character and be confident about himself or herself.

"Social awareness" makes a person empathic. This means that a person is able to recognize the feelings as well as the needs and worries of people around him/her. Someone with this ability is able to recognize even the smallest emotional signs, and can be able to adjust during social gatherings. They are aware that there is strength in the differences between the individuals in the group or in an organization.

"Relationship management: This is a function of one's ability to spot and strengthen existing good relationships, to communicate effectively and be able to inspire others. This means you'll be able to work well in a group and have excellent management abilities.

Emotional Intelligence is a crucial aspect

Emotional intelligence, as a matter of fact sense, is the capacity to recognize the, process and manage the various emotional signals correctly and efficiently. This can be done by an individual , but can also be transferred to other people. The information about emotions can be used to regulate your thoughts and behaviors and can also be used to affect the mood of others.

Emotional intelligence is among the most essential elements for living a satisfying and joyful life. It provides an individual with the necessary tools to apply the core levels of intelligence in relation to emotional responses and allows them to understand that the responses could be rational repeatedly or inconsistently due to certain assumptions about emotions.

As human beings evolve and become more intelligent, there is a growing evidence-based evidence to prove the notion that people at various levels with greater emotional intelligence possess more of the qualities required to work effectively within teams, manage any change that comes in their direction, and deal with the stress. This helps them to be more effective in achieving their goals in business.

Experts have been able discern the primary characteristics that constitute emotional intelligence. They believe that, unlike the intelligence score (IQ) These specific abilities of EI are able to be learned and mastered by those who do not naturally possess it as well as those who possess it may be able to improve it.

While EI is linked to IQ however, they aren't identical. EI is different from all other psychological phenomena that is to be related to some of the attitudinal characteristics which an individual can improve. When you've been successful in working on it, you're likely to reap some unique advantages ranging from wellbeing and happiness to increased levels of achievement in a structured way.

In academics emotional intelligence has been proven to be a huge help to be successful. Also, it is believed that it plays an important role in physical and mental health and is a factor in professional success. An investigation has revealed that people with greater emotional intelligence lead a healthier life than those who's EI isn't as high.

In the 21st century work environment for instance employers continue to put great stress upon the significance of emotional intelligence more that academic credentials.

It is vital to keep one's eyes about the significance of emotional intelligence and to ensure that it is valued. It is a fact that can't be denied. power of being able to be aware of and manage one's own emotions is the very first step towards understanding one's capabilities.

It's difficult to make progress of any kind when you're not able to note your starting point and recognize it. If you're trying to make use of a map to find direction, you'll not be able trace the route correctly if aren't sure the exact location to begin.

Whatever your goals is, whether you are looking to improve your relationships to others through enhancing your interpersonal communication , or are looking to grow in your work environment or build to improve your skills to create interpersonal relationships. If it's managing anxiety or motivation, or working on your decision-making abilities emotional intelligence is essential in helping you achieve the goals you have set in your professional or personal life.

In general, the value that emotional intelligence can bring to the lives of a person is extensive in the pursuit of personal and professional success. It is an extremely important ability to have in all disciplines and can aid in enhancing the chances of achieving the academic and professional goals. It helps build relationships with others and enhances one's communications skills.

The variety of ways in how emotional intelligence aids individuals is. One of the evidences for the value of EI is the fact the belief is that people who have a high degree of EI regardless of ability to perform, have better results in all aspects of life.

There's even an ongoing debate about the advantages of pedagogy within the realm of emotional intelligence. People who belong to these schools of thought put importance on the notion that children who are emotionally intelligent will be emotionally competent adults.

Being emotionally smart is slowly becoming a necessity for longer or more intense forms of emotional work involved with caregiving such as social or nursing work. Management and service positions are also sectors where emotional intelligence is needed.

An analysis by experts shows the fact that emotional intelligence can be tied to the success of interpersonal relationships due to the fact that it is essential to build and develop the foundation of healthy human relationships.

Participants of this research, and who had higher levels of EI and higher levels of EI, were most likely to become sensitive when it comes to taking stances and working with others. They were also more loving and sought to be more satisfied in their interactions with others. They typically had better social abilities.

It is important to remember the fact that health and fitness is correlated to self-awareness, the capacity to manage emotions and stress, as well as interpersonal and personal problem-solving capabilities that are a sign of emotional intelligence.

One who is subjected to stress for a long time and the lingering negative consequences that it brings such as depression, anger, and anxiety are more prone to fatal illnesses such as diabetes, hypertension and heart disease. This increases the likelihood of contracting viruses and infections. In this scenario the wounds and injuries are much more challenging to repair. These issues can be avoided by lowering the amount of stress that comes from emotional intelligence.

The importance of emotional intelligence is hard to quantify. significance of emotional intelligence because it is the primary reason that people are able to develop the positive qualities associated with it, such as determination, communication, resilience managing stress, and many more. These traits all aid in the pursuit of personal goals, as well as professional, physical and overall well-being.

Tips for Improving Emotional Intelligence

A lot of times, people become annoyed with the people around them whether at work or in their interactions with other people. Some even push themselves to the edge that they consider abandoning their job due to the negative relationship.

The majority of the time this happens because from a poor sense of emotional intelligence from a superior, subordinate, or even a friend. Sometimes, it could be that you yourself are the one lacking a awareness of EI. It's always easy to highlight the flaws of others, but how do you go is the point of looking for ways to make yourself better.

Below are a few ways you can develop the emotional intelligence of yourself

Think about your own emotions

Make time to take a break and examine your personal life to discover what you do with your emotions. Be aware of the ways you feel when you encounter situations like:

* You've received an email saying that you didn't win the promotion that you had

* Someone you love blames you for something that you did wrong in a manner you believe to be unfair

* A motorist who stops ahead of you, just before the light turns red

* A loved one or friend is grieving over the loss of a beloved loved one

When you are capable of identifying your feelings in these situations and more, you'll be more aware and will begin working on getting control of your emotions.

Get the opinions of others

Sometimes, we don't recognize that people view us in a manner that is quite different from how we perceive ourselves. It doesn't have anything to do with be about whether people's opinions on us is right or not. The most important thing in this case is to learn the reasons why opinions of others are different from our own and the implications that could result due to these opinions.

You must seek out questions about yourself from people who are close to you. In this way you'll be able learn more about how they view yourself from the way that they interact. This will help you create a new perspective on your own self.

If, for instance, you were in a situation where you were experiencing high emotions, seek out someone else to determine if you behaved differently at the time. You can ask them to write about the manner in which you acted. It will be easier to understand when they are able to relate your experience to previous times in which you also went through a difficult situation. You may ask questions like:

What was my method of speak to you during that time?

* Do you believe I was insensitive to your feelings at the time?

If you can find the correct responses to the questions above, you'll be able to view yourself in the eyes of other people and be able to recognize the emotions of other people better. By understanding this you'll be able to make the necessary adjustments to the way that you interact with others.

Be More Watchful

If you've been able to understand how others view yourself, you should now strive to be more aware of your mood anytime. An amalgamation of your own reflection as well as the opinions of people around of you are enough to keep you attune to your own emotions.

If, through the two exercise, you've gained knowledge about yourself, return to the initial step and think about your own reflections. It is possible to note down the experiences you have had. This can help you make your thoughts clearer and will help you stay open to new experiences.

Stop for a moment

Stopping for a moment may mean taking the time to stop and think before you speak or perform. Your life will be much simpler if everyone does this. Meetings will be much shorter and sloppy remarks in public domains can also be kept out of.

Keep in mind that it's simpler to visualize the pause, rather than actually doing it.

Whatever the case, regardless of whether you're adept at managing the emotions you experience, there are instances when anxiety or an unlucky day can hinder our ability to manage our emotions constantly.

It's not just when things are not going well, and there are instances that we feel compelled to take advantage of opportunities that appear appealing without taking the time to consider the implications. A moment of pause can bring a lot of benefits in these situations.

If you can learn to take a pause before speaking or react, you'll have developed a habit of contemplating your actions before deciding to act.

Think about the "Why"

Most people agree that qualities like compassion and empathy are essential characteristics for healthy relationships. It's a shame that many people fail to cultivate these qualities when they are required most, such as that we do not comprehend our closest friends or companions as they go through difficult moments.

This is what is referred to in the field of psychology as the "perspective gaps." It is a term used to refer to the reality that it is difficult to place ourselves in the shoes of other people.

We often forget the feeling of being confronted with certain circumstances, even though we've had similar situations previously. Even if you've never experienced the same situation consider the possibility that your ignorance of what it's like to be in that situation. This can limit your perception.

Is it now possible to overcome this gap? It's possible. If you have the ability to display traits like empathy and compassion this means you should try as hard as possible imagine yourself in another person's position. In real terms it is more than relying solely on our own experiences to evaluate situations. To show empathy it is necessary to look into the reasons for why:

* What is the reason why the other person is experiencing the way that he is experiencing?

* Why is he/she working on this particular issue?

* Why can't I feel exactly the way he is feeling?

If you're not able to respond accurately You might want to look into having a conversation with the person experiencing the issue for a time to understand the issues he or she may be experiencing and to view it from their perspective. In this way you'll begin to see other people as they really are, and not just as rivals. Being compassionate will enable you identify when someone else is struggling are struggling and in need of assistance.

Don't be offended by criticism

Whatever you're doing no matter who you are, it's never easy to accept criticism. Whatever you are doing it is likely that you've put in many hours of effort, shed tears or bled and sweat to get to where you are now, so it's never a good idea to see someone emerge from nowhere to smear everything you've put into it.

It is a fact that criticism is usually rooted in truth, and that's the case even for the times when it might not have been properly interpreted. If you receive negative feedback about an action you've taken There are two actions you've done: put your emotions aside and gain knowledge from the experience, or get angry and let your emotions take over your life.

If you're the one who is getting the criticism, regardless of whether or not it's being properly portrayed it will be a lot of good to think about any of these:

• Put your personal thoughts aside and consider what you might gain from this viewpoint.

Instead of focussing on the manner in which the criticism was expressed take a look at how you can use this perspective to be beneficial to you by using it to help you improve your own performance.

There are instances when you don't have to hear criticism. A good example is when criticism is based upon falsehood or is made for the sole purpose of destroying your confidence in self-confidence and self-esteem. However, the truth is that this might not be the case all the time.

If you want to strive to improve your self-esteem and be better, you should not allow your emotions to close your mind from criticism. Instead, allow yourself to learn from it.

Rely on leadership Skills

Most people with the highest levels of emotional intelligence are leaders with good skills. They are highly regarded by themselves, and establish the highest standards for themselves and lead lives of exemplary character that others can follow. They typically take on new challenges and are effective decision-makers as well as problem-solvers. This is for their higher productivity levels in general performance. This is also evident in their professional life.

Be friendly and approachable

People who are emotionally smart are always friendly. They always have a smile on their face and emit positive vibes. They utilize their social skills based on their relationships with the people who are within their immediate vicinity. With excellent interpersonal abilities, they are capable of communicating effectively regardless of whether it's either non-verbal or verbal communication.

Be an assertive Communicator

If you can demonstrate a confident approach to communication and a confident manner of communication, you'll be able to win respect from others without appearing as an aggressive or inactive person. The people who are emotionally intelligent understand how to express their opinions or express their needs clearly and yet be respectful of the opinions and feelings of other people.

Respond to Conflicts, Not Reacting

When faced with conflicts, emotional rages and arousals People who are emotionally intelligent are able to maintain their at peace. While they might be anxious, they make sure that they don't make decisions based on their emotions. They are aware that decisions based on impulses could cause more issues for them.

They are aware that when there's an issue, the only thing they must be looking for is a solution. So they are determined to make sure that the right words and actions which can lead to resolution, rather than adding tension to the situation.

The bottom line is that these skills are ideal for those who have a solid understanding of human psychology. While the ability to be emotionally intelligent could be born from the inherent emotions of people with empathy however, anyone can be working on improving their skills. If you aren't emotional need to become more aware of their own behavior and become aware of how they interact with others. When you practice these techniques and observing these behaviors, you'll be one step closer to enhancing your emotional intelligence.

Chapter 7: The Reasons You Have to Take Responsibility and Create Personal Limits

Whatever occurred to you throughout this life time, the fact is that you're the solely responsible. If you're seeking satisfaction and happiness in your professional and personal life, then you need to embrace this concept. If things go badly in life there's always the tendency to blame other people for your problems However, that will not bring you happiness within your own life.

In fact, it will eventually worsen the situation and ultimately lead you into more responsibility. Accepting responsibility for your choices, actions and the direction you take in your life is the most effective and efficient approach to tackle the problems that you confront in your life. If you do not take responsibility for your actions, the perception your life has will change and typically you'll start to think of yourself as a failure due to the fact that you've let yourself blame on others for the problems you face.

When you are fully responsible for your actions, and feel control and joy regardless of circumstances, you're more able to make better choices and decisions as you fully understand that only you, are accountable for the results of your decisions. When things occur that aren't under the control of you, however you are in the ability to decide what you'll do in response to these circumstances. You can choose to either create the most of an event or utilize the difficulties in your life to build an opportunity to climb an even higher stage.

How to Be Responsible

A single of the most important aspects you must accept is that you're in control of your life and that there is no anyone else. Whatever you try to convince others around you that the happenings that are happening right now are not the result of your choices but you'll still have to confront them and accept the consequences when they occur. If you wish to stay in control and manage the challenges you face with determination and resolve then you must follow these steps.

Stop blaming others

If you're by yourself or with others, it is important to pay attention to your own thoughts as you speak. Make sure to get rid of excuses and blame in your words. If you continue to replay the blame game in your head the more likely you'll try to delegate responsibility to others.

Take a serious look at feedback

There will be occasions where you aren't hearing your voice while speaking to other people. This is the reason that accepting feedback from others is essential in your ability to develop emotional intelligence. Certain people you speak to could be honest and attentive enough to share their thoughts about the way you shift blame onto others. If you are willing to take this type or feedback with seriousness, it could assist in changing your behavior and how you view your life. It's not unusual for us to oppose any feedback that isn't in their favor. The more you disapprove of others' opinions the more likely it is that you'll continue to follow your reckless tendencies to your own disadvantage.

Plan Your Life

Your life is the totality of your plans, decisions and actions you make on a daily basis. If you put a strategy that outlines what you would like your life to go you will be able to successfully make decisions about your future and stop being blamed by others for events that you are accountable for. Your plan must be simplified into feasible objectives that you can evaluate the progress you make on.

Recognizing Your Choices

You can make a decision about how to react to any circumstance. This is independent of the seriousness of the situation. There is a possibility to get imprisoned and maintain your mental stability. There is the possibility to concentrate on things that are more positive than the current situation that you're in. This can help you release your thoughts and, more importantly all of your being.

How to Determine Personal Boundaries

Once you begin to recognize what your personal boundaries are and what are healthy boundaries and unhealthy ones it is crucial that you understand how to establish the boundaries. The process of setting boundaries for yourself physical and emotional it will be an exercise that can take time, which is why you must be patient.

Take a look at your boundaries

It's almost impossible to set and set boundaries for yourself in the absence of knowing exactly what those boundaries are. Spend some time thinking about those things that make you feel uncomfortable. Determine the degree to which other individuals can enter your life, and what they can do when they come up to you. This will enable you draw lines of separation that will allow you to determine your personal boundaries.

Express Your Needs

Don't be afraid of letting your friends and family members know what you require to be a part of your daily life. For instance, if you are irritated by the sounds somebody is making, you must be able to inform them that you prefer silence and to take a step back or move to another location. This sends an alert to notify them that they're intruding in your privacy.

Set Consequences in Place

Like any boundary violation, emotional or physical it is essential to have an outcome that is triggered. People can experiment by committing an infraction that is minor to determine whether they are subject to any penalties. If there are no consequences and they continue to intrude into your personal boundaries. In fact, they may even attempt to set up an entirely new code of conduct in communicating with you. It is essential to put penalties in place, like stopping conversations, leaving your space or refusing to respond to stop people who want to breach the boundaries of your own personal.

Stand Your The Ground

If you want to establish and keep your personal boundaries effectively it is essential to stand firm to your ideals and your values and never compromise the boundaries even for a second. When you do make a mistake, and then compromise your position and your values, others will quickly jump in and sabotage your boundaries. The emotional intelligence of a person is evident in the way you handle your charge and determine your own personal space. Someone who has a clear value system as well as an easily-detected set of boundaries is thought to be more competent and emotionally smart.

Chapter 8: Identifying Your Strengths and Weaknesses

It is possible that you have noticed in interview that one of two most common questions that you will be asked is to inform interviewers what you are good at and where your weak points lie. This is a deliberate practice. If you believe that you're perfect, don't believe that you'll be hired. It's a sign you aren't aware of emotional intelligence. People with this type of intelligence are conscious of both their strength as well as their weaknesses, yet they do not let their weaknesses hold them behind. Since they know about them they put forth a greater effort to work on areas they believe to be weak.

The method I'm about to recommend is that you take notes on a notebook and record your strengths. This can include your character traits and relationships strengths, as well as the skills which you believe you excel in. There is no limit to what type of abilities they are. You might be a pro at drawing, or maybe you excel at solving mathematical problems. Whatever your talents you're good at, you must recognize that because those with a strong emotional intelligence recognize their strengths and make use of them to be successful in their professions and lives. Make the weaknesses you have and be completely honest. It's not easy to do this however, if you don't doit, you'll not be able to discern what areas of your life require improvement. If you are truthful, you can work on any of your weaknesses one at a time and build your ability.

The most emotionally intelligent people also know their limits. This includes recognizing that something cannot be an ability. Let's take a look at the kinds of things this refers to:

All actions that are beyond your control.

All aspects of yourself which you cannot alter.

Acceptance of your limits is important because you aren't able to increase your height as an example and there's no point in focusing on it. Certain limitations can be found in everyone's life, but once you realize what they are and decide there's no thing you can do to change them, you must to accept them. In to achieve this by rebutting your strongest aspects against those you consider insignificant and inflexible helps to be able to accept your own uniqueness. The issue with all of us is that we have the option of accepting your own self or insist on a certain appearance you present or how you behave in certain situations. If there are things you can't alter, you must accept them because there's nothing is possible to do with it. People who are emotionally intelligent realize this and don't worry about the little things. They also realize that it's counterproductive to live based on desires. Accept yourself for who you are since the sooner you accept yourself the more easy it will be to offer yourself to other people in a more comprehensive manner.

Question your livelihood

Once you have figured out the strengths and weak points of yours, can you confidently affirm that you're at the right place in your career? It could be that you're wondering if the position you've been offered is a temporary fix and doesn't necessarily match your abilities in any way. It could be that you're not able to be successful because you're average at the job you've chosen to work for. The most emotionally intelligent people seek out jobs that bring them satisfaction, even if the job you are in doesn't make you feel happy, it might be the time to tailor your abilities to the task you've chosen to work at. I'm not suggesting that you abandon your job until you've been able to look at the other options available. It is important to be honest and understand that bills have to be paid. If however, you realize most of your day is doing tasks that have no meaning for you, it's time to change your life and look for something that is more significant. Do not give notice at the place you work until you're certain that you've found the right job.

This is just one part that you have an emotional intelligence. Ask yourself questions about your life. It is important to be honest , and the next questions to ask are:

What number of people have made my life more enjoyable?

*Am I patient and compassionate with other people?

Am I critical of other people in a reason that is justifiable?

The next section we'll discuss how you react to others . We also provide exercises that will help you improve your relationship with other people at work and out of the office. It's crucial to tackle this chapter by keeping an open-minded mind and be prepared to make adjustments to your behavior to enhance your emotional ability.

Chapter 9: Becoming Acquainted of your own emotions

The first step to harness the potential of emotional intelligence starts with your own emotions. Becoming more in control of your emotions, and projecting confidence in yourself can reassure your employees that everything is under control. Leaders who are not disciplined will exhibit anger and frustration, particularly during times of stress. That isn't exactly a positive character trait of a leader, and shows the lack of their emotional ability. You should be able to control your negative emotions and convey positive emotions.

How to manage negative emotions

The times are hard You're stressed and your entire office is on the verge of a deadline. You schedule a meeting to discuss a new strategy and develop a new strategy to meet your goals. You can choose to conceal your negative feelings or let them be displayed during the meeting. People are aware of when pressure is on and deadlines are coming and observing an employee in a state of stress isn't an indication of confidence. As an administrator, you need to ensure that you're the source of confidence that your workers can trust. If they feel they're not confident in themselves or your company's image, they will turn to you for advice and support. It is not possible to do this when you display the negative emotions they feel.

The ability to control your emotions isn't something that is easy and requires a lot of discipline. It is important to be able to focus and present confidence. Making a plan with a focus on numbers you must meet in order to accomplish that plan is one method by which you can reduce your stress. anxiety. Spend some time walking around or re-readjust your thoughts before speaking to your employees. It's fine to let off tension and anxiety in a private space but remember not to let your employees see your sweating. Maintain a positive outlook that inspires confidence. You will be able to see a strong and ready workforcethat is eager to join you in the battle.

Inspiring and Motivating With Positive Emotions

Although you'll want to stifle all negative thoughts when you're managing, the opposite applies to positive emotions. Your positive feelings should be able to flow and truly inspire your staff. If you're a dull person who is shy, you must make a change if you're planning to be an emotional leader. People react positively with positive feelings and are naturally drawn to people who are positive and outgoing. Look at your social circle. The person with the most popularity is the most active and positive member of the group. Look over the self-help and motivational coaches. They scream onto the stage with positive feelings as they play music that is pumping and each phrase they use is delivered with enthusiasm. The energy and excitement is infectious and could influence your staff or your guests. Be sure to bring an element of enthusiasm to your leadership style as it can help a lot.

Assessing Your Strengths and Strengths and

One of the characteristics of someone who has a high degree of intelligence in their emotional state is that the fact that they know what they are good at and weak points. Leaders with emotional intelligence are able to recognize and exploit their strengths and strive to reduce or enhance their weak points. Self-improvement is a characteristic of the best leaders and you'll see that the best managers are seeking to improve in all aspects of their lives. You must create an honest evaluation of your leadership style if want to be an effective manager. Make an outline of the top 10 strengths as well as your most 10 weaknesses. For each strength, you should write down how you can showcase your strength, and make sure that you are using it to its maximum potential when taking charge. Each weakness should be noted. notes of ways you can minimize the weakness, and also what steps you'll make to transform this weakness into strength. The most successful leaders acknowledge their weaknesses and take every step to ensure their weaknesses do not affect their leadership way of life. If you have to call an additional hand or seek guidance Strong leaders aren't willing to hide their flaws.

Creating A Confident Environment

If you want to be able to handle your emotions and emotional intelligence, you'll have to establish a secure setting. This step begins with the person you are. As a leader or manager, you will make crucial choices, and you'll need to be sure that you're decisive as well as confident. You should present a confident and positive image even when you have doubts about your decision. Managers who are new struggle to be confident when they face situations that they've never encountered before. This could lead to an uneasy work environment as well as conflicts in the signals given by the manager when he is giving instructions.

Chapter 10: Emotional Intelligence

Conceptualizing emotional intelligence (EI) or emotional quotient (EQ) was developed through the work of earlier researchers, specifically Peter Salovey and John Mayer. It was not widely accepted up until Daniel Goleman, an American psychologist, introduced the concept in his book entitled: "Emotional Intelligence - Why It's More Important Than Intelligence" 1995. In the years since, acclaim of the concept has increased and is growing more crucial as we progress as a nation. His prominence was a major reason emotional intelligence caught the attention of psychologists from other fields and the general public and prompted further studies and studies.

The first question that pops to your mind is: What exactly is emotional intelligence? Emotional Intelligence refers to the ability to detect, comprehend the signs of emotions, to understand and control the emotions of others and one's own. In terms of definition, EI is simply the capability to:

* Identify, understand how to manage and control our personal emotional state

*Recognize, comprehend and influence the moods of other people

This sounds straightforward and simple. However, it's not an easy task and is an art that needs to learn consciously. Individual efforts must be made in order to get a an understanding of the idea.

To a greater extent the things that happened to us during our lives is something we can't influence, though there's always another way. However, the best part is that we are able to influence how and to what degree these life events influence us. How you deal with disappointment or failure is dependent on your emotional ability. Sometime, those suffering from extreme emotional stress may are tempted to commit suicide. The thoughts of suicide may linger in their thoughts. Since the thoughts in their heads are constantly popping up in their heads, they keep receiving incorrect answers whenever the time comes. This could affect their judgement and it is no wonder why they are able to put the unplanned into action later on.

The level of emotional quotient differs among individuals. For some, even the slightest hint of arousal can trigger their apprehension and others will need the roar of a more powerful and violent breeze to move. But being emotional intelligent is not something you can acquire or a talent, nor an inherent talent or a trait that can be passed down through genetics. It is a skill that must be learned and learned; after all, the place which we live in is our classroom!

Emotional intelligence is a decision. It is possible to not have the skill.But it's safer to possess it since it gives us a second arsenal to deal with the challenges life throws our way. It is crucial to have emotional intelligence because we as individuals, our achievements as well as the longevity of our work/career in the present depend upon our capacity to discern the signals of others and react effectively to them.

To achieve this it is vital for each of us is able to build the maturity of our emotional intelligence abilities to better understand communicate, empathize with and negotiate with other people , especially since the world economy is becoming more global. If we don't, success may not be available to us in our careers and lives.

Emotional Intelligence - Elements

Daniel Goleman formulated an outline of five essential abilities that define emotional intelligence. The five skills could be paired with two core abilities that include personal competency (Dealing within yourself) and interpersonal or social competence. (Dealing with other people)

Personal qualities

*Self-awareness

*Self-regulation

*Motivation

Interpersonal abilities

*Empathy

*Social skills

Self-awareness: This refers to the ability to understand your feelings and how they impact your life. It is about paying focus on your surroundings as well as your body and your mind. It is crucial to personal growth. It provides you with a deeper awareness of your own personality and the way you relate to others. When you're aware of yourself and aware, you are paying attention to your values, feelings as well as your habits, personality desires, emotions as well as your strengths and weaknesses. You are aware of your self and a clear understanding of who you really are. It can also assist you recognize your feelings and how they can be stimulated. Similar to that the process of developing self-awareness is paying attention to your emotions. This is based by the idea that when you examine your feelings, you are able to manage them. Additionally you will be aware of what your threshold is. In the true sense there is a truth to the saying that every person has a breaking point since there is an amount or limit to which we are emotionally exhausted. If we reach the limit the person could be broken and, when stretched too far, it could break.

If you are prone to a flare-up You should have the notion of your own limits and focus on taming the anger that is pulling you from your calm self. If something or someone has you pushed towards it you should have realized that it's a signal to take a step back or find a way(s) to get around it. This is self-awareness. Self-awareness is a crucial ability for personal growth and good interpersonal relationships. If you're self-aware, you will have a better understanding of who you are as well as how you relate to other people. This makes you pay close at your own feelings about your values, life style, character emotional, needs strengths and weaknesses. You are more aware of yourself and a profound understanding of what you're about. You are aware of the things that have an immediate impact on you as well as the people who surround you. Self-awareness is a skill that can result in greater happiness in life, more positive decisions, and ultimately greater achievement in our private as well as professional life, and even as parents.

Self-regulation linked to self-awareness because you need to be aware of your triggers and breaking points in order to be aware of what, how, and when to manage the triggers. Simply put, it's about keeping in control, and mainly aiding yourself in deciding against something that happens automatically when you are subjected to certain situations.

As an example, suppose you're prone to apprehension to the temptation of soda even though your doctor has advised you to not drink it, because of a specific health condition. Self-awareness is already present that is backed by your advice of your doctor however it requires an effective level of self-control to avoid giving in to the desire to consume the drink when it's being served at a party with a friend. Self-regulation could prompt you to drink water , however, not soda.

It is also evident that one has very little control over what one feels emotionally you can learn an ability to control the length of time an emotion will be lasting by employing a variety of techniques to lessen negative emotions, such as depression, anxiety or anger. Certain experts have identified strategies that are used by people at different moments to cope with the situations, such as changing the perspective of a situation to an optimistic way and taking a long walk and praying or meditation. They have also suggested that self-regulation is based on the following characteristics:

Self-control: Managing disruptive impulses

Honesty: Upholding standards of honesty and honesty

Responsibility: Accepting responsibility for your own actions

Change-making: Managing change through flexibility

Innovation; Be willing to try new concepts

Motivation A motivating instrument in human endeavours. It keeps us connected. Do not be averse to those who keep you connected. so, having a thorough understanding of your own motivations is crucial to achieving an emotionally stable and wise state.

However, it's important to remember that motivating yourself to achieve any accomplishment will require clearly defined goals and a positive outlook. Although it could be the case that you have the predisposition to adopt either positively or negatively mental attitude. In reality, when you are a human because of a variety of factors and circumstances, you can through effort and repetition develop a positive mindset by identifying negative thoughts before they happen and reframe them into more specific phrases. This will assist in numerous ways to achieve your goals. So motivation is comprised of:

Strive for excellence: Trying to make improvements or reach an expectation of excellence.

Involvement: Complementing the mission of the organization or group.

Initiative: Being prepared to take advantage of opportunities.

Positive outlook: Keeping pursuing goals despite setbacks and obstacles.

Empathy: As a rule humans tend to critique even the smallest flaw that we discover from someone or something. The one flop that is a failure gets all the attention, while the rest of the thousand tasks that are that are done well get brushed under the rug. If we take time to reflect on things that happen within our lives there will be less confusion. Empathy refers to being able to recognize the feelings of others regarding the situation.

Empathy is when you put on someone else's shoes. If you are able to walk just a few kilometres within it you'll be slow to make a decision and judge. As someone once said, "If you are offended and on the verge of losing it all then find a reason to explain the reason before you realize that, your thoughts are focused on the cause and the anger has been gone. In the end, there exist three perspectives to any story you're on the side, theirs; and the truth. If you take the time to connect the two sides and gain a 3D perspective and it becomes apparent to you that your reaction might not be needed. Many of the confusion can be eliminated by simply spending the time to learn another's perspective in advance of trying to persuade them to accept your view.

How to Enhance Your Empathy

You can't give away what you don't and there's no way to create compassion from the void. Empathy begins with you. it is essential to start practicing compassion for yourself by seeking out your emotional needs while recognizing when it's feasible and when it's not, and then swerving against the current when needed so long as you're able to manage the circumstances.

Be attentive to your the way you move your body. Your body speaks more about the way you feel about an event than your voice. When someone crosses their arms or move his feet forward and back or bites his lips without speaking It means something. The gesture signifies that certain things are going on in the mind. Watch out for signs that indicate you wish to comprehend the thoughts of others more effectively. This can assist in responding in a way that is appropriate to the situation.

Be aware of the emotions of others: As emotional quote is the sum of the way you feel and what others (around you) are feeling, try to comprehend what they are experiencing before you take action.

Social skills: No matter what the circumstances, one needs to be able to handle a difficult task. Be open to positive feedback in addition to negative ones. Life is unpredictable. In addition, how you interact to other people is crucial.

Enhancing Your Social Skills

To improve your social skills, you need to keep practicing the behavior consistently. At first, it might be difficult but after a few years of consistent training, it will become automatic and effortless. In the field of emotional intelligence, the core of social skills is being adept at bringing people together, and to sacrifice your comfort to gain the benefits of the others. Concentrating on what the team would like to see. It is easier to be motivated by the brilliance and achievements of others, not of yourself since when you push someone to the limit it is impossible to see how they'll be any better than you. Social skills are about knowing how we interact with others.

Chapter 11: Inspire Motivation

Another crucial way to aid in controlling the psychological environment in the workplace is to encourage motivation. One of the most common reasons for anxiety and stress in the workplace is the lack of motivation. If employees are feeling overwhelmed unappreciated, undervalued, and generally dissatisfied about their work, they be unable to find the drive that drives them to put forth their highest effort. The result isn't only a poor performance but also a decrease in motivation for the task to be completed. In addition is that the longer someone is demotivated and is stressed, the more unhappy they are by having work that doesn't bring them joy. So, motivating yourself is crucial to creating an atmosphere that's positive for emotional wellbeing.

Furthermore, you can help others develop emotional intelligence who are around you by generating motivation. If you teach people how to deal with the pressures and stress in the workplace by your actions, you can aid them in create better habits and behaviours that are their own. They will build emotional intelligence without conscious of that they are doing it. It's important to always show emotional intelligence in what you do and say and set the bar for others to emulate.

Set the example by leading

There are numerous books about the various styles of leadership, as well as the benefits each one has. One thing that all books explain that is how important it is to being an example to follow. Although it may seem like an idea that is revolutionary however the truth lies in the fact that each manager leads by example , whether they know it or not. If a leader reacts too strongly to every setback they experience, they'll inspire all employees to behave the same way. The reason is that managers propagate the perception that setbacks can be devastating when they react the way they react in this way. So, even if they aren't intending to, they increase the anxiety and stress in their workplace by responding in an emotional manner.

This makes sense once you consider that human beings are just as from animals in terms of learning. All animals learn by following and imitating the behaviors of their parents or other animals. This is the way that birds learn how to swim and ducks are taught to fly, and lions are taught to hunt. While we learn new skills in schools or by using instructions, the observational process continues. This means that people learn behavior and abilities in response to what they see as well as experience any other method. This is the reason being a role model is important for controlling the environment that is emotionally affecting any space, not just work.

When you are aware of the benefits of modeling behavior you can then begin using the method to gain and also to the benefit of the people in your circle. The first step is to be proactive about avoiding negative behaviour. It's not enough just to never be seen to be in a negative mood but. You must also be able to take the initiative to avoid and denounce it. An example is how you respond to defeats. If things don't go according to plan, you have to be able to demonstrate your emotional intelligence through your response to the circumstances. Instead of becoming stressed and screaming, be confident in your ability to competent to resolve the issue in front of you. Also, show that you don't view obstacles as an issue initially. This will show that your confidence isn't an illusion that conceals the truth of your emotions.

Another method of leading by examples is setting the standards for ethics and morals. You cannot expect your colleagues to be punctual when you're always late or in the wrong time. If you show up to the office on time every day, and you have your tasks completed before their deadlines You will inspire others to concentrate their efforts to be punctual. In addition, being honest is essential to create an environment that is positive and emotional. When you're honest with your peers, you inspire others to be honest about you. This will greatly reduce the anxiety and stress caused by dishonesty, insincere actions, and other similar elements that only harm an individual's emotional stability.

Recognize hard work and achievers

Numerous studies have demonstrated that a different method to instill motivation in an individual is to reward hard-working and achievement. Most of the time, the primary stress in any workplace is on the consequences of failing. Many employers believe that the best method to ensure that employees be at their best is to ensure that the risk of being fired for a failure ever present in their minds. This approach has been found to cause not just unimaginable anxiety and stress however, they also weaken the performance of a person instead of increasing it. In the end , it appears that a negative attitude only produces negative outcomes.

It has also been observed that when individuals get rewarded for their perseverance and accomplishment, they perform better regularly. This is an important aspect to be aware of in relation to the psychological wellbeing of people near you, especially at work. Each time you reward someone for good behavior you'll encourage them to behave exactly the same way. This applies to any element of performance. When you show gratitude for an accomplishment you can encourage someone to keep performing at their very best. The reason behind this is that happiness always outweighs fear in the battle to motivate. So, you must always be generous when rewarding those who perform excellent performances and achieve positive outcomes.

One of the main benefits of rewarding the hard work of others and their success is that it creates the sense of teamwork in any workplace. The primary reason is that people are conscious of fact that managers are prone to be awarded bonuses when they reach their targets. The reality is that the average employee typically is left with nothing regardless of their efforts and hard work to achieve the objective. Then sharing the fruits of success with the people who made the difference initially, it makes employees feel more an integral part of this process. The more valued employees feel they are valued, the greater their contributions will be which will lead to greater results.

Chapter 12: The Eq Fitness Program: Workouts for the development of Emotional Intelligence

Emotional intelligence is the growth of skills such that allow one to comprehend both their personal feelings as well as the emotions of those who are around. Because of this we are able to effectively control reactions to the emotions of others and, consequently perform our tasks more effectively. The most important thing to do to develop emotion intelligence does not mean to ignore or suppress difficult emotions or feelings however it is important to manage the emotions and feelings.

It's the emotional intelligence that makes successful leaders different from everyone else. Managers who have high levels of EI are more efficient when it comes to hiring new employees, inspire colleagues more effectively and can be efficient in the service industry. Emotional intelligence is crucial regardless of the stage of your career, particularly in the event that you wish to attain an exemplary level of accountability in your job. As well as in other areas of your life, EI allows you to be healthier, happier and build stronger relationships. So , how can you enhance your emotional intelligence and let it benefit you?

1. Create awareness of one's emotions

People can be affected by their emotions, causing them to behave in a strange and, often, unproductive way and self-awareness improves your ability to comprehend how you interpret and perceive your personal feelings moods, moods and inner motivations. This will allow you to identify the emotional state of others and comprehend the motives the motivation behind their words and actions. In a nutshell, if you aren't able to comprehend your own motivations and actions, you'll not know what others are thinking.

What should you do:

Three times a day, repeat three phrases which begin with "I feel" ..." and I am feeling." With this method, you'll slowly be able to identify your emotions and improve self-awareness.

Every day, take the time to feel the emotions you've experienced - write down what you feel and the reasons behind it.

Be aware that emotions can change and are only last a short time, so they can't be used as a basis for communication or decision-making.

Consider the negative emotions that - like angry, rejection, or disappointment or jealousy affect your coworkers and clients.

Determine your needs and fears. This will allow you to better discern what is bothering you and what is driving you.

Examine how you respond to stress. Are you angry each time something doesn't go in the way you had planned?

2. Self-control for emotions

It is essential to build the ability to manage impulsive emotional reactions that can negatively impact your performance and leadership. The next step following the growth of self-awareness. Self-control, in short, can be defined as the capacity to go "higher" than weak explanations, jealousy, or breakdowns and not let emotions influence your actions. By exercising self-control, you'll be able to think before you act, and earn a credibility as a reliable participant in any group.

Self-control techniques:

Do not take sides with one side or the other in office dramas or conflicts.

If the situation is emotionally challenging and tense, take a break for a bit and don't take a decision immediately. Review your feelings.

Accept the reality that life can change and that frustration and anger are a part of every job. The professional response to these situations can be "brainstorming" and devising strategies, not complaining or suspension from work.

Do not participate in the "find the one who is guilty" game. Do not blame everyone and everything around you. Learn from your mistakes and admit your mistakes.

Keep your focus on you and the things you control, and stay away from things beyond your control.

Find ways to react to emotions that don't involve spontaneous reactions or insensitive expressions.

3. Enhance your capacity to display empathy

Empathy is an innate process to build self-awareness and emotional awareness. It helps you move away from your personal situation and to see the issue from the perspective of someone else. Through developing empathy, you demonstrate the ability to treat people with dignity, respect, and professionalism. People who are compassionate are adept at being able to recognize the feelings that others feel, even when they're not immediately apparent.

The best way to develop empathy

Follow the golden rule: treat people the way you would like to be treated.

It is not difficult to maintain your viewpoint and be guided by this sense Put yourself in the position of someone else and examine the situation from the perspective of his.

Learn to pay attention and reflect on what your partner said to you.

Every day, at least Ask how someone is feeling, for instance on a scale of 1 to 10. This will help others to let their emotions be known and better understand them.

Accept the worries and fears of others - let the person know that you understand their root and appreciate the importance of their viewpoint.

4. Find motivation

Motivation is a drive and enthusiasm for your work and professional life that cannot be explained with financial or social status. It is what makes it possible to reach your personal goals and accomplish it with remarkable persistence.

Motivation: How to increase it

In any situation that is difficult or even if you fail Try to find at the very least one positive aspect.

Take a picture of the moment when you are thinking and speaking in a negative manner. Pause, and then "scroll" through your head all the thoughts and phrases. Make them positive even if you have to pretend to be.

There is a tendency to lose sight of you are truly passionate about your job. It is important to take the time to write this down, as well as the primary reason you should be aware of the work you do.

Keep in mind that people are drawn to energetic, positive and motivating people. If you boost motivation, you'll receive more attention from your colleagues executives, top managers, and clients.

Set yourself up with inspiring and , at the same time, set achievable goals. Create a list of the tasks that must be done in order to meet these goals. Recognize yourself for achieving the main objectives.

5. Improve your communication skills.

A key aspect that is a part of EI is its capacity to be able to communicate effectively with others, however it doesn't mean shy people or introverts aren't able to communicate. EI. Communication skills can come in many forms, as it's not just the ability to be welcoming and friendly, but also the capacity to listen, persuade the other, and use non-verbal and verbal communication abilities. Managers who have an emotional intelligence that is high are usually adept in communicating, resolving conflict and sharing their ideas with their team They set the behaviors as well as values others emulate.

How can you improve your communication skills:

Find out how conflicts can be resolved and the solutions. This can help when dealing with difficult situations between colleagues, customers or suppliers.

Be sure to praise your colleagues to inspire your team and make them more loyal. Be sure to know the person you're speaking to. You can't have one method that is applicable to everyone in the office.

Chapter 13: Taking Emotional Intelligence To Work

The impact of emotions is huge on workplaces. This is by far the most emotional workplace you'll be in during your career. It's filled with negative emotions like anxiety, stress, depression and a drive for competitiveness which will affect not just the way you think , but the way you behave. It is unfortunate that many people allow their negative feelings at work to dictate their emotions which can lead to numerous regrettable decisions that lead to serious problems. This could result in losing a job. You can utilize you emotional influence to deal with situations that are threatening, such as a boss who is rude or a grumpy coworker, as well as unprofessional subordinates.

Within this segment, we'll examine the connection between leadership and emotional intelligence in the way that crucial interpersonal skills are linked to emotional intelligence.

Aspects of EMOTIONAL intelligence that are required to be A EFFECTIVE LEADER

The ability to work in synergy with your emotions and self, as well as being in control over an event, is a powerful skill an effective leader must have. Emotional intelligence means knowing, comprehending, resolving emotions and being aware of how your behavior can affect others, and the ability to manage anxiety in difficult situations is what makes you a leader.

To become a leader of excellence it is essential to know what is emotional intelligence.

Self-regulation: The ability to control your behavior and manage your emotions that cause disruption and be able to adjust to the changing environment to keep everyone on the same path. The ability to be calm can be infectious and, as an executive, you can't be able to let yourself panic when faced with difficult circumstances. If you're confident and calm you'll be able to think clearly and better communicate.

Empathy and compassion is the ability to be sympathetic to a situation to comprehend what they're feeling to be able to respond and act accordingly. Empathy will make you be more than just a little more. The emotions you experience when you see someone in need drives you to assist the person in need. The stronger the connection you share with those who surround you, the more you'll know the things that make them feel happy or sad.

Controlling your relationships: If you're distracted, then you'll be unable to establish deep bonds with other people. Everybody has a hectic schedule however, the ability to establish and sustain a healthy relationship is vital to improving the emotional intelligence of your. It is essential to effectively communicate to keep relationships in order to lead people around you to the correct direction.

Effective communication is essential for connecting with people. Research has proven the communication process is comprised of 70% of what you say and 93% is your body language and tone. The most common cause of miscommunication is of conflicts between people, and a failure to communicate effectively results in bitterness, frustration and confusion. By utilizing an effective communication strategy, you will be able solve issues and create stronger relationships.

EXPANDING HIGH-SELF-AWARENESS

On a typical day you may have to speak to an angry customer, respond to a boss's angst or present an idea at an interview. The way you conduct each of these tasks can be influenced by a variety of variables. If, for instance, the angry customer is making one ridiculous request after another, you may be irritable with him. If you're confident in your part in the project, you'll likely be able to ease your boss's worries. If you think your colleagues believe you're not experienced enough to do the job and you feel embarrassed and uneasy when the presentation of your ideas at a conference.

Being aware of your behaviour and feelings and the actions of the captions that others have of you, may affect your actions so that they serve to your advantage. In the first instance, you realize the client you are dealing with is driving you nuts You also realize that distancing him from him can have disastrous consequences. Your best option could be to calm him down rather than annoy the client with your erratic temper. In the second scenario one, the boss who is stressed, when you feel that she is due to the fact that much is dependent in the accomplishment of the particular project then you may make sure to tell her about your actions and reassuring her that your idea will be accepted by the boss. In the final scenario If you're conscious that your colleagues perceive as unexperienced or untrained, then you'll need to be prepared prior to making your presentation.

The most important thing is to tune to the abundance of Information your thoughts, emotions, senses and appraisals, as well as your actions and motives available to you about you. This helps you comprehend the way you behave, react and communicate in different circumstances. This is what we refer to as self-awareness.

REASONS WHY EMOTIONAL INTELLIGENCE IS VITAL FOR LEADERS

As leader, you must to possess emotional intelligence because it gives you a variety of abilities like building relationships, inspiring people, and inspiring them, and the ability to bypass social media.

Here are a few reasons why that a leader should possess emotional intelligence

Self-Awareness A leader who is self-aware, they can easily identify emotions within his surroundings, and that makes him more effective because they know the right solution. It is essential to possess as leader because it provides an understanding of what your weaknesses and strengths are. If you are aware of your own weaknesses it is easy to handle emotions as they come up.

Management of emotions: This means you can control your emotions and keep them under control. If you are able to control your emotional state, you're likely to not make decisions too quickly and let emotions take to the top of your head. In order to be successful in your leadership position it is essential to remain in control of your emotions in check.

Effective communication: Being able to use your communication skills allows you to express clearly your thoughts as well as what should be said and done in order to encourage or motivate those who are under your supervision. Your team's ability to listen and efficiently complete tasks is heavily depend on the ability of you to communicate effectively them.

Social awareness: When you have an impressive degree of intelligence in emotional matters, you'll be able to comprehend the feelings of others and be aware of the circumstances that surround you. This assists you in dealing with any challenges that arise efficiently. If you're looking to motivate and inspire people as a leader, you must be aware of social situations. If you aren't able to empathize with your employees, you will not get the respect and trust from your workers.

Conflict resolution: Conflict and risk are part of the work environment If they are not managed properly, they could affect the effectiveness and productivity of the workplace. As the leader, if have the right emotional intelligence, you'll be able to resolve disagreements and offer resolution to disputes.

CONTROLING THE ENVIRONMENTAL IMPACTS IN the workplace

As was mentioned previously it is an extremely emotional place, and you need to know your feelings and the feelings of your coworkers. It is true that emotions can be influenced by external circumstances like actions and words are affected by emotions. So it is crucial to keep an eye on the emotional environment since if it is not monitored this can lead to increased levels of anxiety and stress, which the emotional intelligence will not be capable of overcoming.

A more positive and uplifting environment can be created by keeping an open and positive conversation with everyone to establish systems and routines which reduce stress levels whenever it occurs. By implementing this approach positively you can turn the most challenging workplace into one of contentment, satisfaction and satisfaction.

REDUCING STRESS and FEAR of failure

One of the main factors that contribute to negativity at working environments is the quantity of stress and pressure that is experienced. Unfortunately, stress is not removed from the workplace so you need to implement certain measures to reduce stress and improve the overall working environment. One way to decrease stress is creating realistic expectations. It could appear as if a person is multitasking when they undertakes a number of tasks, but the reality is that many people are overwhelmed when this happens repeatedly. It is advised to never create unrealistic deadlines and to never undertake tasks that are too big to take on.

What is the significance of emotional intelligence In the workplace

Emotional intelligence is an essential ability because it enhances the management of relationships, communication and solving problems. Research has proven that with continuous training and practicing emotional intelligence can be improved. Here are some additional reasons why emotional intelligence is crucial for working environments.

The performance of the workplace is heavily dependent on interactions with people

A typical business employs a wide range of workers comprising of different skilled workers. They collaborate with the same goal to achieve. The reason they are able to collaborate with the same goals in mind is due to their understanding. Collaboration is about understanding each other and establishing and sustain important relationships. It's also about the capacity to manage oneself and to self-motivate oneself to work effectively together in order to achieve the greater goal. The term "emotional intelligence" encompasses all of the above as well, and if it's not functioning in the smallest of workplace interactions it could be a sign of certain issues.

It is a crucial element of leadership

The leader is accountable for all materials and financial resources that are at his at his disposal. The most valuable resource is human capital, and how they are managed will affect the effectiveness of your organization. It is essential to develop people skills because it allows you to show and develop a sense of emotional intelligence. Understanding the emotions of people and how they can be used is one of the main components of EQ. Empathy is a crucial talent, and when tapped on , can create loyalty. When you are aware of the way people think, you'll be able to make better choices, and you will be more appreciated as leader. If you recognize your limits and your potential, you are able to effectively manage your workload to ensure your stress levels remain to a minimum and you're a more effective leader.

It is a powerful recruitment Instrument

After reviewing all credentials and credentials are verified HR managers will test the applicant's emotional intelligence in order for determining if the individual is suitable for the job. In an interview, candidates should be scrutinized to see if they align with the values and goals of the organization. Interviews for jobs have questions that aid the HR personnel determine whether the applicant is emotionally competent.

The High-EQ Workplace Workplace

You'll be able to make better decisions and be able to solve issues

You'll keep your cool even under pressure.

You'll be able deal with conflicts better

You will feel more empathy

You'll be able be more attentive, reflect, and react to constructive criticism more effectively

The low EQ of the Workplace

You'll play the part as the victim, or you will not assume the personal responsibility for your mistakes

You'll exhibit aggressive or passive communications patterns

You'll not want to be a part of an organization

You may be too critical of other people or willing to listen to other's opinions and opinions

Emotional Intelligence and Job satisfaction

It has been extensively studied and has been proven it is connected to satisfaction at work. People who have high emotional intelligence are also likely to have higher job satisfaction. It is because they are more relaxed when there's positive emotions at work, as opposed to those who experience negative mood. Positive emotion boosts motivation and drive to do their job and assists to increase productivity. The more productive the employee and greater the efficiency of the business or organisation is. This will make the employer happy and may even give the worker a reward. The employee will feel appreciated and content about their work.

The ability to be emotionally intelligent at work can help employees;

Work stress better and manage it.

Develop your relationships with your coworkers.

Be more effective with your boss.

Be more productive.

Improve your management skills and become a better leader.

Better manage your work priorities.

Be more effective as a team player.

All of this assists the worker to be more satisfied working. Additionally, since those with high emotional intelligence are more aware of the environment and people in their workplaces, they tend to receive higher pay increases.

What happens when there's an absence of emotional intelligence at work?

There are two ways in which a deficiency of emotional intelligence could negatively impact work:

Communication without emotional intelligence communication can be a frustrating task at work. You will find many people speaking but nobody listening. There is lots of miscommunication in the workplace as a result of confusion. Emotional Intelligence is the ability to communicate the right message at the right moment and in the appropriate manner.

Decision Making In the absence of emotional intelligence, decisions is prone to error. This is why it's an essential skill for top-level management and executives. In order to be able to make the right choices it is essential to be emotionally knowledgeable.

How emotional intelligence impacts communication in the workplace

If the emotional intelligence of employees isn't there at work this can lead to many problems, including:

There is no understanding of emotions.

There is no understanding of the emotions of other people

Ineffective or inadequate or effective communication of thoughts and feelings to other people

Unsporting behavior and poor communication that can trigger outbursts emotions, excessive sharing or not communicating important information.

Examples of EMOTIONAL Intelligence in the workplace

In terms of being productive and determining the success within the work environment, the emotional intelligence of employees is believed to play a significant part. Research has proven that individuals who have higher emotional intelligence have higher productivity, possess higher social abilities and have higher success rates than those who have less emotional intelligence. Being able to demonstrate emotional intelligence at work significantly improves productivity. These are the finest instances of emotional intelligence in the workplace environment that you must be looking for.

Give a sympathetic ear and angry colleague The truth is that every employee is a human being, which means that they will experience an off day at times and isn't invincible from feeling annoyed. As an administrator, how you handle your employees reveals a lot about your emotional ability. When you're kind as well as understanding of others, it indicates that you are a person with a excellent emotional intelligence. If you are conscious of the emotions of others this is a sign that you recognize that everybody experiences fluctuation in emotions every now and then and you are aware that the feelings of others are important.

Inviting people to speak their mind In other words, if you allow individuals to express their thoughts and express their feelings without fear of reprisal, then you've got a place of work that is highly emotional. When there's a respectful exchange, emotionally intelligent individuals do not get angry when a individual's opinion differs from their own.

Flexibility: Allowing your employees to be flexible with how they work could be the key to keeping your most productive employees and maximizing your profit. A leader who is emotionally intelligent understands the changes in demand and is able to work with his staff rather than restrict how they perform their work. The most emotionally intelligent leaders do not hold everyone to the same beliefs or set of priorities.

The ability to be creative: Certain positions require high levels of imagination. It's understandable to find a an ideal match between talented people and a creative company. A business that practice emotional intelligence provides employees with to have space, time, and the freedom to think creatively and help the company achieve its objectives.

How EMOTIONAL INTELLIGENCE IMPACTS DECISION MAKEN IN THE WORKPLACE

Emotional intelligence is essential at work, since it aids in making decisions. When you have a high emotional intelligence, employees can recognize the cause and effects of emotions and they'll be able to make effective plans.

However in the event that emotional intelligence can be low, then there could be a variety of emotions that can occur which can cloud their judgement and decision-making. For instance anxiety is a typical emotion that can affect making decisions. Those who have low emotional intelligence may not be able to identify the cause of their anxiety, and how to deal with it effectively that can result in dangerous decision-making.

Employing EMOTIONAL Intelligence to manage and resolve issues in the WORKPLACE

The use of emotional intelligence is numerous in the workplace, however there are three main areas where emotional intelligence can be efficient and include:

Management and leadership

Management of projects

Social work

Emotional intelligence does not only apply to these three domains, and is applicable to every aspect of work. Team coordinators need to know the meaning of emotional intelligence since it aids working as a team and in the effectiveness of performing tasks.

Chapter 14: Self-Management

Do you wish to become a boss? What would you do when I said it was possible to manage the operations of an organization and get paid for it? If you think you're capable of handling the job There are some things you must know. First, the organization you work for is made up of you. The person you are is composed of a variety of important elements. Your thoughts, feelings and memories, your habits and rationality, as well as health desires, relationships and more all come together to define you as an individual human being. How you decide to deal with the external and internal factors that impact you on an everyday basis determines how you live your day. How much you can enjoy happiness or experience regret, it all depends on the ability of you to be the person who is in charge of your life.

The other thing to be aware of is that certain competencies are necessary to effectively manage your life. If you do not have these abilities, the areas in your life listed above may not be able to hand the control that control your lives to you. Many people live the entirety of their lives governed by relationships, emotions and mistakes from previous experiences, as well as other. They are guided by instincts and make uninformed choices that add to the errors they'll regret in the near future. These abilities are described in the following paragraphs and constitute the qualifications you show yourself to prove the extent of your emotional ability. This might sound odd to you right now, however looking at self-management from this perspective provides the proper view.

Learn the Skills for Self-Management

Think about these as the essential skills you need to master before advancing to a more advanced course , or the required qualifications to list on your resume when you are looking for the job. They aren't impossible and have been proven for their effectiveness in self-management. Learning these abilities will give you greater control over your actions with less guilt. These skills aren't in any particular order.

Responsibilities

Refraining from challenging tasks and failing to learn from mistakes made in the past are indications of inattention. As children, we and our teachers and parents attempted to instill this trait in us. For some, it was enough to make them accountable and some had to learn how to be responsible from the experience itself. But, there are people who have escaped all the lessons, in believing that they were unimportant. However, they discover that not many people want to work with an unresponsible person. Businesses, investors as well as lovers are all looking for people who can keep a check on their moods and actions. Who would you trust who is known for shifting blame even on occasions where they're responsible?

Being a responsible individual means that you're eager to learn and work hard to organize your life and acknowledge your flaws without pointing fingers. People are attracted to you when you're accountable since they know that you are able to add value to their lives. This isn't selfish of them. Many people are seeking their own personal development, and they are in need of someone who can assist them but also support them in return.

Self-preservation

The ability to stay alive and away from anything that could be detrimental to our existence is component of every animal's instinct. As strong as the lion's instincts are it is, it has the ability to recognize danger circumstances and take measures to avoid these. Self-defense is a human trait that extends beyond the limits of these. We are aware, for sure that knives and fires could cause death. What do we feel about sleep deprivation and binge consumption of unhealthy food items, insufficient exercise, and apathy?

If you aren't allowing yourself enough rest each night you are unlikely to be you will be a productive person. It does not matter how clever or motivated you may be. If you're continually taking your time sleeping at some point, you could end up getting distracted, exhausted and reducing your productivity.

Consuming junk food is always like fun and harmless initially. You might not even be concerned when you see an increase in weight. Over time, it becomes clear the Big Macs and doughnuts could cause overweight, which is one of the main causes of death across the world.

Training is a process that requires effort and pain. Building muscles is not an easy task. It's a process that requires sweat, aches and weeks of intense working without noticing any changes. You just need to continue working in a consistent manner, monitoring your diet closely and not getting discouraged.

If you're looking to be an interesting and valuable person and be a valuable person, you must be someone who questions and is seeking answers. Insanity is a good thing but it is also a sign of the mediocre and unfulfilling. It is a good thing that we live in an age where information is readily found on the internet. Videos and books have been made available to people who want to look them up.

Initiative

Certain circumstances require us to wait to be informed of the actions to do. It doesn't matter if it's the military or in politics, or even in business. There are hierarchical structures that should be observed. However, this isn't always the case in all situations. As the structure changes in companies and evolve, people who aren't unwilling to take on new challenges are sought-after. Sometimes , you might be gifted with an idea, but you would be required to act as swiftly as you can, and nobody in your company might be willing to manage it under their supervision. If you take initiative at that moment will show that you're indeed enthusiastic about the growth of your company. All you need is the famed outside-the-box thinking and the determination of bringing your concepts into reality. Your ideas may not be innovative or effective. Certain things seem more appealing in our minds and on paper than actually. However, you must be prepared to look over each of them, try them, and then put them into practice. If you're working in a place that doesn't encourage creativity and you prefer to do everything by yourself If so, you might be thinking about getting out of there. Making decisions without being directed helps you discover the possibilities of your own potential.

Stress Management

You might want to boast about the amount of professional that you have been to buddies. They tell you that you don't take a break and how little sleep you have and how over-stressed you are. The reality is that stress is harmful to your physical as well as mental well-being. The ability to think rationally and with a sense of logic can't be expected from a person who is stressed and it's certainly not something that you can be proud about. A lot of health problems are attributed to a life of stress. Whatever how busy or intense the world could be, it's important to take time to peace and relaxation. Here are a few suggestions to help you reduce stress in your daily life.

Sometimes, we feel overwhelmed by how crammed life is. You're faced with deadlines to fulfill and appointments to make and obligations to keep in mind. However, other obligations come into your life and create a mess that you feel like drowning in. The safe word to keep your life from this disaster. However, refusing to be a part of the conversation doesn't come easy for all. Many people are caught between a need to relax and a need to please others that they take on more responsibilities than they are able to manage. This is my suggestion to anyone who is one of them. It's nice that you care about hurting others' feelings and want to assist in any way you can. But what's the reason you would be tempted to hurt yourself? You're as much of an individual as any other human being and, at the end of the day you are all you really are. Give people respect, but remember yourself the most important thing. What can you be should you get sick because you are overly stressed?

Have you ever returned home from work and needed someone to chat with? It's not like people around us can take the burden off of our shoulders. They can listen to our stories of the day however, it can be distracting and enjoyable. One of the best remedies for stress is to find at the very least someone who you can talk to about things. Stress can trigger other emotions like fear, anger and suspicion as well as feelings of urgency that are not real. Finding someone who isn't too busy to hear you, look at the world from another viewpoint and give you sound guidance is an absolute blessing. The person you choose could be your lover, your parents, a friend from your past or an therapist. You only need the one person with whom you are comfortable enough to express your feelings and to find the rest that you require. And, someone who can give you the information you need to hear, in contrast to what you believe you want to be hearing.

The stress we feel could just be the body trying to guard ourselves from danger. Although the likelihood of encountering wild animals that want to devour us in our everyday life is extremely rare however, we still have to deal by situations that can threaten our peace. An imminent deadline can cause the fight or flight action in our brains. But due to our sedentary lifestyles the stress lingers present even after the danger has passed. Certain chemicals are released when we experience stress caused through fear. They make our bodies more prepared for jumping, running or other physical actions. Exercise is an excellent method to aid your body in become more relaxed, by utilizing the stress hormones released by the brain. There is a rare feeling of the need to exercise particularly when we're not as fat like the average person. Eyes alone can't be relied on to gauge the need to exercise. Join an exercise center, buy exercise equipment, take the stairs instead elevator, or simply take a walk in the mornings.

Your diet can be one of the factors that can cause you to be stressed. If you're the type of person who leads an active lifestyle and consumes every kind of food with no discipline, then you'll likely to get overweight. Stressing about your body image and the condition of your health will not reduce anxiety. In addition to drinking alcohol, which is harmful for the internal organs of your body as well, it can also be depressant when consumed in large quantities. Drinking excessively can cause you to feel depressed and unmotivated. Sugar is another ingredient that we often consume in large quantities. The first time we consume it, we experience an immediate increase in our mood, but it doesn't last long. The energy boost that comes by eating sweet foods dwindles quickly feeling depressed and causing us to seek out more sugar. This can lead to a cycle dependence that can lead to depression as well as other health problems. Sugar is supposed to consume in small amounts and should gradually be diminished as we age. Beware of the use of nicotine or other addictive substances. They provide only a brief increase in energy levels as our bodies aren't prepared to handle the sudden crash that occur after a few days.

The time of night for most of us is the time when we engage our minds in making plans and worrying about the events of the following day. We lie awake staring at nothing as our minds imagine various scenarios, usually the ones that could happen. The thing we don't always realize the fact that anxiety and rise in blood pressure aren't an outcome of a hectic life. Stress can create sudden spikes on blood pressure. Even though they only last for just a few seconds, the repeating of those spikes in blood pressure can cause damage to some of the main organs of the body. It is normal to feel tired at night due to the fact that our body is taught to utilize the time to heal itself and recharge itself to face the demands of the following day. Insomnia or anxiety prevents this from happening, and could result in something more serious than blood pressure rises and hypertension.

To prevent this from happening to reduce stress, download relaxing songs with no lyrics and concentrate your attention on the sounds rather than worrying. Make sure that your space is a free area. There shouldn't be anything within your home that brings back memories or can cause you to feel stressed. Shut off the television and switch off your mobile If you have to. Relax your body and mind to receive the rest they need.

Meditation is among the most effective methods to reduce anxiety in our lives. Instead of exercising and allowing the body to release the adrenaline that circulates through the bloodstream, meditation puts the body to relax into a calm state. Instead of your mind getting lost in thoughts of worry it is possible to focus your focus on the rise and decrease of your breath. Instead of exhaling reflexively while inhaling and exhaling can consciously take control of that movement. This can lead to lessening the speed of heartbeats and normal blood flow and the risk of developing hypertension. Choose a peaceful area with the least amount of objects that could distract you. It is possible to pick any position however it is recommended to lie down. It could be crossed-legged in the ground, or in the lotus posture, or on chairs. It is also recommended to have an alarm set while you are meditating. The need to glance at the clock every second minute is not a good idea for those who don't want to get distracted. Ten minutes of meditative time is typically enough to control blood pressure, decrease the rate of metabolism, and put things in the proper way for anyone. You can choose to sit for more time than that but it is contingent on the amount of time in your hand and your desire to go on for a longer period of time.

Skills for organizing

It depends on the ability of you to maintain things in check and set prioritization. Human beings are not naturally multitaskers. Our minds must be focused only on one task at any given moment for us to be productive. Yet, our lives are typically full of more than one thing that we have taken on. In these situations, we need find a way to finish those projects and perform at our top performance. That's where the ability to prioritize and organization abilities come in handy. The most intelligent people in the world are planners. They are prone to think ahead, anticipate and plan strategies to face any problems they could face. They are aware of how unpredictable life can be, and are prepared to modify the plans they've laid out in response to any changes that occur suddenly. They design and follow routines to ensure that their lives are running smoothly and ensure that they're focused on the aspects that really are important.

A routine can be beneficial if it's beneficial in helping you become more efficient. Certain routines are nothing less than habits that can take valuable hours or minutes from our lives. If you have a routine schedule for getting up to brush your teeth, working out at your gym at home, bathing and cooking breakfast, consider whether there are any specific things you do during the time that you can get rid of by. To stay organized it is important to plan your schedule to give yourself enough time to complete the essential and urgent tasks.

The use of a notepad, either via an app on your smartphone or as a paper-based form can be a great asset for any person. The ability to recall information quickly and in the appropriate time isn't the same for all. In general, human memory isn't something to be relied on 100. While we can remember things in the moment, it is likely that we be unable to remember certain crucial details. This is why everyone requires a notepad. You should have a notepad that is easily accessible on that you can record tasks, appointments as well as other essential activities during your day.

Due to the amount of work we do in the day, and how exhausted we are when we get home, it can be a hassle to tidy up the place they belong after we've used them. There are times when we leave our clothes scattered around, throw keys on the sofa or even fall asleep. Finding a space for everything and carefully sorting your clothing in a certain arrangement isn't something that is only reserved for those with a disorder called compulsive. In reality, anyone can take a leaf of their book to declutter our lives. That means that some things within your home would need to be removed particularly the ones that are only useful because of sentimental value. Once you have done that, put in an effort to organize and maintain order for each object. This will prevent you from searching for the right item or recall where you put your keys to your car as you rush to get to work.

There is a saying that the only way to make something happen correctly is to complete it yourself. If that is true, then you could think that you must do everything yourself. It's not just unlikely that you'll possess all the skills required to perform a variety of tasks however, there are only a certain amount of hours in a day to become an accountant manager, sales manager, or accountant and also to manage all for your accounts on social media simultaneously. It is possible that you will require the assistance of other experts to accomplish the task quickly and efficiently. This is referred to as outsourcing. If you manage a business and you decide to recruit within your team, it's called delegating. Many hands could cause a mess, but having the right amount of skilled and experienced hands will ensure that you're not anxious trying to do it all on your own. It is possible that you will need to oversee the actions of all members of the team but don't take it too far. Allow them the freedom to lead and express their own creativity.

Chapter 15: The Social Management and Responsibilities

The most rewarding thing is knowing that one can talk and make clear sounds and words to describe emotions, events, and things.

Camillo Jose Cela

The terms "social management" and accountability refer to a group's or company's involvement in ethical, environmental, and social issues that are not within the institution itself. "Outside the organization" could be a reference to issues that are at the national or B2B (Business to Business) level, or even the personal development of individuals within the group or the organization.

The benefits of emotional intelligence

Emotional intelligence refers to "the ability to detect emotions, be able to access and generate emotions in such a way that they aid thought to comprehend emotions and the emotional world and to manage emotions to encourage the development of intellectual and emotional intelligence (Mayer-Salovey, Four Branch Model of Emotional Intelligence).

It is important to focus in the value of Emotional Intelligence and acquiring EI skills can bring many advantages. Particularly, it impacts one's capacity to make decisions, relationships and overall health.

Decision-making. Being aware of your feelings, where they originate and the meaning behind them, can help you take a more rationaland organized approach to the way you're going to make a certain decision.

Relationships. If one can comprehend the reasons for being in the way they are and the reasons they react to certain situations in like the way they are, they will tend to gain more appreciation for the people around them and who they are. This could be a catalyst for greater relationships, both in personal and professional.

Health. In many cases, internal tension manifests as physical illness. Being constantly afflicted with negative emotions can cause more stress levels in the body, and this can cause irreparable harm to it.

Express your emotions using language

When you were a child you may feel it is acceptable to "act out your feelings to make your point However, once you are an adult, it's looked down on and definitely not acceptable in the workplace. Your emotions will never cease but it isn't an excuse to talk that, or act the way we'd like to. It is crucial to know your feelings and what they mean and why you feel this way And then, share your emotions through a positive and constructive dialogue.

If you are in a leadership position there are many occasions to express yourself, whether you are applauding a worker's job accomplished, or warning employees for not meeting deadlines. However, the most important thing to do to make sure that you express your emotions effectively and in a timely way is to channel those emotions in a way that is clear and professional.

Practical Illustration

Katie realized that the levels of emotional intelligence in her workplace were not as high. To improve them levels, she held a conference to discuss their importance. She explained that emotional intelligence can have an impact on the business in general as well as the individual employees who are the ones who run it. If every person is educated on decision-making and has good habits in the relationships they have, as well as a general control over their stressors and anger, they will be emotionally well-educated. When they worked on these areas the office became more in its ability to handle conflicts from both sides and growth, resulting in the development of a more successful company.

www.ingramcontent.com/pod-product-compliance
Lightning Source LLC
Chambersburg PA
CBHW071840080526
44589CB00012B/1070